Beyond

*Exploring the Frontier of God's
Expanding Revelation*

Garris Elkins

Beyond: Exploring the Frontier of God's Expanding Revelation
© 2020 Garris Elkins

Prophetic Horizons
PO Box 509, Jacksonville, OR, 97530 USA
info@prophetichorizons.com | www.GarrisElkins.com

ISBN: 978-0-578-63431-9

Now to Him who is able to do far more abundantly **beyond** *all that we ask or think, according to the power that works within us, to Him be the glory in the church and in Christ Jesus to all generations forever and ever. Amen.*

—Ephesians 3:20-21 NASB, emphasis mine.

CONTENTS

ACKNOWLEDGMENTS

Mark and Margie Simon—thank you for a friendship that has become a prophetic laboratory for personal and cultural reformation.

John L. Moore—in your great craft as a novelist, you affirmed and encouraged me to write about my personal family history of pioneers seeking a new life on the Applegate Trail. I am grateful for your wisdom and friendship.

Anna Elkins—my daughter and ever-faithful, wise editor. None of my books would have become a reality had you not been present. I love you dearly.

Jan Elkins—I put you as the last person on this list because, along with God, you are my foundation—my trusted, resting place. When you read what I write, you become my soul-editor. You know me best and won't let me settle for less. I am forever yours.

WHERE ARE WE GOING?

This book is about the stages of our life journey that lead us to the frontier of God's ever-expanding revelation on Earth. Whether we are on a personal journey or a shared one, we will experience distinct roles and seasons. Understanding those roles and seasons will give us purpose, definition, and clarity.

Under the mandate of The Great Commission, God has released a heavenly blueprint to align each nation with His plan for them to flourish. His Kingdom is joy, peace, and everything that is good and right. There is no end to the increase of His government and His peace. His Kingdom is always advancing (Isaiah 9:7). Jesus is inviting the nations into His prosperous heart of joy and peace and righteousness.

You have a unique part to play in that endeavor. I invite you to let God define your role as you discern your season in this Kingdom adventure.

I'll begin by sharing the beginning of my own journey, and then I'll share the things God has taught me along the way.

CHAPTER 1: BEGINNINGS

I grew up in the Santa Clara Valley of California. Our family settled there before it became known as Silicon Valley.

My mother and father met in San Francisco where my father worked on the construction of the Golden Gate Bridge and Treasure Island. As newlyweds, they made their first home in Richmond.

After I was born, my parents felt a nudge to move out of the increasing crowds and urban sprawl. They looked south to the Santa Clara Valley. My contractor father bought two lots on Dardanelli Lane in Los Gatos and built two houses on spec. One of those houses became our family home for the next 23 years.

Growing up in pre-development Silicon Valley was heaven on earth for my brother and me. Our street only had homes on one side, and our house looked out over an expanse of fruit orchards. Right in front of us was Mr. Dardanelli's orchard. I grew up with those trees always in my sight and mind.

In the springtime, our family took drives up Blossom Hill Road to look out across the valley at mile after mile of blossoming orchards. When the blossoms began to fall, it looked like a snowstorm had carpeted the valley floor.

I could hike for miles through orchards of plums and apricots. Each school day, I could not wait to get home, grab my trusty Daisy BB gun and head out into the orchards to explore. Dirt clods became bad guys who fell to my copper-colored BB's. Trees became my shields as I ducked for cover in pretend shoot-outs. And the corridors of fruit trees became the imagined lands of faraway places.

The orchards of my youth are long gone. The Santa Clara Valley is now covered in fences, tract homes, and asphalt parking lots. But anyone who had grown up in that valley before the orchards would have remembered it as even less developed than when I was a boy.

In November of 1769, the Spanish explorer Gaspar de Portola and his exploration party camped at Point San Pedro to heal up from sickness. Two soldiers left camp to hunt for deer. They climbed the mountains and described the valley before them like an inland sea, stretching as far as the eye could see.

These two men, whose names were not noted in the historical record, stood on a summit of the western foothills overlooking what would someday become known as the Santa Clara Valley, named by Father Junipero Serra who founded the mission at Santa Clara.

As a boy, I looked toward the summit where those hunter-explorers from Portola's party once had stood. Even at a young age, I was drawn to distant summits. I imagined how passage could be made across a faraway mountain range to reveal yet another summit and another passage onward.

I wondered about those people who had explored the land before my arrival. But of course, the land had been inhabited long before those Spanish explorers.

I remember the day my Dad brought home an ancient grinding stone. A subdivision of new homes was replacing a walnut orchard in Morgan Hill, and Dad's backhoe had dug up the artifact while trenching a foundation. These grinding stones were used by the Ohlone people, who predated the arrival of European explorers by thousands of years.

If that construction was happening today, we would

have stopped and invited archaeologists to the construction site to honor and preserve the evidence of a previous civilization. Back then, I'm sorry to say, we just kept digging. Each time I walked by those grinding stones in my mother's garden, I felt a sadness I couldn't name and a curiosity about the people who had come before us.

Early explorers, like Portola and Drake, scouted into unexplored regions, looking for resources and potential. Later explorers, with names like Jobs and Gates, scouted new routes into unexplored technologies that would eventually change the name of my childhood valley.

While the Santa Clara Valley is still known on maps as such, its new name in colloquial terms—Silicon Valley—has gained worldwide recognition as the technology capital of the world.

With every step of exploration, we bring new definition to old territory. And we add our history to the history that came before us.

Like my parents, I also migrated after marriage and my first child. In 1977, my wife Jan and I moved north to Oregon with our one-year old daughter. My new valley of residence was the Willamette Valley of Oregon.

That migration would be the first of many for our family. On and off for the last 40 years, Oregon has been our home. We have orbited in and out on various assignments that took us to other states and nations, but our anchor point has always remained Oregon.

In 1999, after four years of working in Europe, Jan and I returned to Oregon, and we've been here ever since. Only after this final return did I discover the significance of this State in my family history.

By 2002, Jan and I had settled into the routine of

pastoring a local church in Southern Oregon. We kept Fridays as our date day. It was important to protect one day as "ours" to maintain our relational equilibrium in the middle of the daily pressures of ministry.

As Jan and I were getting ready to enjoy our date day one week, I suggested we visit The Applegate Trail Interpretive Center. We had sped by it on Interstate 5 many times before but had never stopped to explore.

The museum is located just north of Grants Pass in Sunny Valley, and it presents the history of the Applegate Trail from its inception in 1846 to the present day.

The Applegate Trail was the southern alternative to the section of the Oregon Trail that traced the wild and undammed Columbia River. Those early pioneers wanted another route into the fertile settlements of the Willamette Valley for two reasons. One was British control of the Columbia River by the Hudson Bay Company. The expanding footprint of the young United States into British territory was creating war-like conversations in the region.

At the time, if you were traveling to "Oregon," you weren't referring to the State we know today. In the mid-1800s, Oregon was a vast territory comprised of Oregon, Washington, Idaho, and portions of western Montana and Wyoming. It was large and wild. Oregon's current borders were not finalized until 1859.

The second reason for creating an alternate route to the Oregon Trail was danger. When the early wagons entered the Columbia Gorge, many pioneers tied their wagons onto crude log rafts to float their family and belongings down river toward the settlements that would someday become cities like Portland. But many of these early pioneers drowned in the turbulent waters of the Columbia River.

In addition to the dangerous rapids of a powerful river, travelers faced disease, injury, and attack. One account of the Oregon Trail claimed that that for every 50 yards traveled, a body is buried somewhere along the trail.

A new route was needed—one not along the Columbia River but overland from the south.

Two men, Jesse Applegate and Levi Scott, were commissioned to scout and blaze the new trail for the coming pioneers. Both men had lost friends and family members on the traditional route along the Columbia.

To scout a new trail, Applegate and Scott headed south, roughly along the line of present-day Interstate 5 to Ashland, Oregon and then south-easterly toward Klamath Falls and south of Lakeview. Many old trapper trails had crisscrossed the wilderness, but this exploration was raw.

East of Goose Lake, they crossed over the Warner Mountains before entering the deserts of northern Nevada to intersect the Humboldt River. From there they made a final push eastward to meet hundreds of wagons gathered in Fort Hall, Idaho. Those wagons were waiting to complete the final leg of their pioneering journey into either Oregon or California.

When they arrived at Fort Hall, Applegate and Scott met the waiting wagons and made their appeal about the new trail they had just blazed. Those who accepted the invitation become participants in the historic Applegate Wagon Train of 1846.

After Jan and I visited the Interpretive Center, I was intrigued by the history of the Applegate Trail and started some casual research. I was surprised to find the passenger manifest for the wagon train.

Halfway down the list of travelers, I saw a name that caught my attention: Alphonso Boone. He was the grandson of Daniel Boone, the historic American frontiersman. My mother's maiden name is Boone, and Daniel Boone is my uncle—many generations back.

When I saw that family name in the passenger

manifest, I choked up. I have always wanted to know more about my family history, and this discovery was an unexpected gift—a sense of belonging that not only linked me to pioneering history but also to the very place I now called home.

God had sovereignly placed me in a region where my ancestors had pioneered, and I had no idea of that when I moved here.

Less than a mile from our home is an historic cemetery where some of my ancestors are buried, each with a link to the Applegate Wagon Train of 1846.

If your travels ever take you north through Oregon on Interstate 5, as you approach Portland, you will see signs announcing Boone's Ferry Road. When Alphonso Boone arrived in the area in 1846, he and his family started a business ferrying people, freight, and wagons across the Willamette River. Years later, cars would be ferried across the river until Eisenhower's interstate freeway system was created in the 1950s. A freeway bridge was then constructed, spanning the river and bringing an end to the ferry business.

The summer after discovering my family history in Oregon, Jan and I took part of our summer vacation to retrace the path of the Applegate Wagon Train. Before our trip, I bought several books detailing the history of the Applegate Trail. I poured over historic documents, maps, and diaries of those early Applegate pioneers.

The records tell of a hazardous journey involving such difficulties and dangers that it was a miracle anyone survived.

I didn't know it at the time, but studying that westward expansion became the groundwork for this book.

That history was a lens through which I could see my past and envision my future. My imagination expanded with new ideas and entrepreneurial adventures that only emerged as I stepped onto the unexplored edge of God's expanding blueprint.

CHAPTER 2: DEFINING ROLES

In every Kingdom endeavor, we have specific assignments that define our role in the process of exploration. To describe the nature of these assignments, I'll use the metaphor of the westward expansion of the United States during the 1800s, including my own history with the Applegate Trail.

Each westward migration consisted of three roles: scouts, pioneers, and settlers.

SCOUTS EXPLORE & PERSUADE

The westward journeys of the 1800s began when a scout headed out to discover a previously unexplored route toward a new destination. Scouts returned from their ventures and invited people to make a journey with them, based on the intelligence they had gathered. They found safe passage through dangerous mountain terrain and across swollen rivers. They took risks that would reduce the risks of those who followed.

In a spiritual context, scouts explore the edge of a fresh revelation where an apostolic blueprint is being considered. That is what John the Baptist did when he cried out from the wilderness announcing the approaching Kingdom of God in the person of Jesus Christ. That is what Paul did when he returned from his missionary journeys. That is what scouting entrepreneurs do today when they explore a new product, technology, or government program.

Along with the knowledge scouts gain during exploration, they must also possess the gift of informed persuasion to convince prospective pioneers to follow them along the trail. They issue an invitation to others, asking them to entertain the risk required to follow a new route toward a promise.

PIONEERS LEARN HOW TO SURVIVE

Most wagon train journeys began in the spring in order to travel during the summer months. It was critical to arrive at their destination by early fall. Once they arrived, pioneers would only have a few weeks to construct crude cabins before the season changed. They had to learn how to survive the first winter, or they would not live long enough to settle the land.

Some lived through their first winter holed up in a drafty wagon. Often, their shoes and clothing had worn out or rotted off during the journey. They learned from mountain men and indigenous people how to make clothing and moccasins from animal skins. Everything was immediate and short-term during that first winter. There was very little rest in a cycle of on-going threats to life. It was exhausting

Like the early pioneers of the American West, some of what a present-day pioneer brings with them at the start of the journey will become worn out from use on the trail or be discarded along the way to lighten the load. To navigate challenging terrain of new product development, a family transition, or a business that has run its course, some things have to be adapted or left behind.

These pioneers will need to be re-clothed with new ways of thinking and new methods of operation in order to complete the journey and survive the first winter season. They must be willing to off-load the weight of assumption.

When the children of Israel entered the Promised

Land, it was a place of promise, but not without hardship. That first generation of pioneers had a journey filled with things that could kill them if they were not willing to fight for the promise.

A pioneer is a survivalist, but not in hopeless desperation. This is surviving with a promise in mind while waiting for spring to come. In the spring, forests can be cleared, crops planted, and permanent homes constructed. Pioneering is about knowing how to survive until spring arrives when a sense of permanence can begin.

SETTLERS CREATE COMMUNITY & CULTURE

Once a pioneer arrives and survives the first winter, they become a settler. Pioneering is a temporary role. Once settled, the pioneer's role transitions into settler. The settler begins to build a sustainable community and culture.

Settlers in the American West created social structures, government, housing, transportation, and trade. Those elements would lead to the long-term, socio-economic health of the community. And then those established institutions created a stable influence on following generations.

If pioneers do not transition into settlers, they will not see the promise they carried with them during their difficult journey.

Just as true, all Kingdom endeavors must transition from pioneering to settling if they are to have a sustainable impact. Unfortunately, people often romanticize the pioneer role, thinking it is a forever lifestyle. But if pioneers don't transition, their influence will eventually die off from exposure to the harsh elements that surround the new thing God wants to accomplish.

The three unique assignments of scouts, pioneers, and settlers are present in the life of any enterprise, whether starting a business, establishing a new direction for civil government, or discovering a new genre for a recording artist.

Everything of lasting value and impact will involve an on-going process of scouting, pioneering, and settling. This is how original ideas and products develop multi-generational lifespans.

It is vital to know what season you are in. Each season has a purpose and a role. Defining these will clarify your message and its application—and help you lead others toward their destination as well.

CHAPTER 3: PREPARING FOR DEPARTURE

Collective learning is the ability to pass on information in a kind of shared memory across generations. Such learning was especially useful in times of human migration.

When our ancestors arrived to an unfamiliar place, they had to learn to overcome new obstacles. They often encountered hostile environments. They had to figure out how to farm in unfamiliar soil and communicate with people who shared a different history, language, and culture. Each layer of newfound knowledge contributed to the collective learning of subsequent generations.

In the last few centuries, humans have been able to connect with each other through more expedient forms of travel. Our migrations have increased with great speed and have covered large swaths of the globe. But at first, these migrations were slow. People walked across land bridges and continents. Then they acquired animals they could ride upon and eventually hitch to wagons. Those early forms of travel were followed by automobiles, airplanes, spacecraft, and now something new.

We currently have at our disposal the fastest vehicle of migration ever known to humanity: the Internet. We are moving at warp speed through time and space, exposed to differing worldviews and ideas previously isolated within a specific culture and not easily accessible on a global scale.

Our current technology has migrated past the first generation (1G) of wireless technology, through the terrain of 2G, 3G, 4G, and now into 5G.

Collective learning has even formed what is called the "global brain," the collective intelligence of humanity. The global brain is collecting, storing, and retrieving data at blinding rates of speed. God is going to use this global brain to shift every sphere of culture—not by force but by a Spirit-directed process of influence that will lead to renewed ways of thinking across the world.

Futurist David Houle wrote a book called *The Shift Age*. Houle said that in the twenty-year period of 2017 to 2037, we will experience more change than in any fifty-year period in human history. We are currently experiencing that shift—and it will accelerate the rate of our migration.

With that kind of rapidity, we will need to continually redefine and streamline our message and mission. We need to be able to move alongside the increasing tempo of culture in order to remain relevant. That relevancy is not the result of compromising our ideals, ethics, or truth, but to better communicate our message.

In the following chapters, I hope to show that life and work are both best accomplished from a place of rest. Speed and rest are not contradictory elements. They are the result of having our mission so simplified that we can actually rest as we move at the speed of revelation.

We should not be encumbered by non-essential issues that cause us to lag behind in this shift age. We have not been called to labor under the load of unproductive ways of thinking and short-sighted programs that do little to accomplish our global Kingdom mandate for cultural transformation.

The mission of transformation is to displace anything that would cause a culture to believe anything less than God's original intent of goodness for creation and humanity.

We were given the Great Commission to help cultures flourish under the influence of God's Spirit: to believe that goodness, not despair, is His preferred future for them.

THE ELEVATOR PITCH

God wants to capture our imagination. In our rapidly developing cultures, one way we can simplify the content of our message is to create a captivating elevator pitch. In this way, we can capture people's imagination—inviting them to the mission.

You've probably heard of the elevator pitch before; the idea is that you hone your message down so that you can deliver it in 30 seconds—about the time it takes an elevator to get between floors. I often ask myself: can I share a simplified concept of God's Kingdom while moving between floors in a chance elevator meeting?

Recently, a mutual friend introduced me to a gifted film producer whose work has been associated with several Emmy-Award-winning productions. After that introduction, Joseph (not his real name) asked if we might get together and talk.

A few days later, we met at a local coffee shop. As our conversation began, Joseph informed me that he is an inquirer in matters of faith. I appreciated his honesty and transparency.

About half an hour into our conversation, I sensed a nudge to share with my new friend what I was discovering in my current season of life. I told him God was simplifying my message and mission. I shared about the different spheres of cultural influence, along with the five equipping gifts Paul mentioned in Ephesians 4, and how those gifts are being used to create a new sound in each sphere of culture.

I knew I was speaking to a significant player in the world of arts and entertainment. I tried to speak without religious terminology; I am always looking for new ways to communicate that will engage people without sounding overly theological.

After I finished sharing, Joseph leaned across the table and said, "I want in on this! How can I be part of what you just shared?"

In the next hour, I fleshed out in more detail what I had shared in brief. In the elevator pitch, I was functioning as a scout, inviting the film producer to become a pioneer and venture into a new season of his life. Joseph's attention had been captured. Without a condensed expression of the mission, I would not have engaged his imagination.

Since that conversation, I have been able to connect Joseph with several friends to engage in future projects together. They are using technologies that will open new doors and opportunities for transforming culture, especially in the area of arts and entertainment.

If we are not prepared and alert, the divine connections God brings our way can be lost between floors, as the conversational elevator moves up and down. If our concepts and resulting conversations cannot move at the speed of cultural change, we can be left behind when the elevator door opens and our audience departs.

The prophet Habakkuk said, "Write the vision; make it plain on tablets, so that a runner may read it" (Habakkuk 2:2 NRSV).

We've got to keep these revelations simple. So simple, they can fit on a tablet and be read while on the run. We can't do this as a scout if what we are carrying requires a moving van to haul the content of our message.

A scout wisely crafts a simplified and persuasive presentation for pioneers who are about to commit life, limb, and resources to a new venture.

When we are considering new options, we don't want to hear an encyclopedic presentation. We want a simple word of hope that something better is possible.

When we are presenting new options, hope must be part of our report before we ask someone to make a choice to buy into God's invitation and follow a new way of thinking and living. We were created to be part of something significant and world-impacting as we partner with God. That is what will capture someone's heart.

REDISCOVERING ORIGINAL CONTENT

In my book *The Leadership Rock*, I wrote about simplifying in the chapter, "End with the Beginning in Mind." I shared an encounter that had shifted my life paradigm.

Twenty-five years ago, I was in Indianapolis for a training event and had the pleasure of talking with Dr. Bob Logan, the presenter. Bob is well known in church circles for developing some of the best leadership training and church planting materials around.

During one of the lunch breaks, I sat at a table with Bob and several others. As the conversation progressed, I asked, "Bob, what advice do you give to individuals or organizations who have plateaued or are in decline? How do you help them get moving again?"

I asked this knowing that Bob is very gifted in evaluating the effectiveness of individuals and corporations. People use his advice with great confidence.

Bob's answer was interesting. He said, "The first thing I ask is this, 'What was your original vision?'" He went on to say most leaders are able to recite their vision in great detail. Bob would then ask a set of questions to determine if the leaders were still functioning in their original vision. Within plateaued or declining corporations and ministries he saw a common thread: each one had stopped doing the very thing that brought them success in the first place. They had ceased doing their original vision.

Bob then shared a powerful truth, "Each time someone rediscovered their original vision and began to do it once again, in each case, without exception, they began to move forward and grow."

I sat there, wonderfully stunned by what I just heard. The conversation continued to move around the table, but I was still processing the words, "in each case, without exception."

In the late 1980s and early 1990s, many pastors in America hung out in the business sections of their local bookstores. In those aisles you could find books about swimming with shark-like people, searching for excellence, creating wealth, and one-minute approaches to every aspect of business. All the titles were verb-oriented—action-oriented. We all wanted to get things moving, so we devoured the concepts contained in these books.

Stephen Covey's book, *The Seven Habits of Highly Effective People*, was especially popular. Covey helped guide people into more productive lives. Most of us read the book and implemented its concepts into our personal lives and workplace. Covey's points made sense. For many years, these principles served us well—and they still do.

There are a lot of good life-plan programs out there. Covey is now one among many. But what I have come to realize about life-plans is that they work best in the long term if they are built upon a word from God. The development of an effective plan must follow a word of revelation. Such words are not found in the business section of a bookstore.

If the plan is to work, it must rest on what God brings to light. In the middle of the night, when doubt and fear come visiting, it will be the word of the

Lord—not a plan—that will bring us comfort.

One of Covey's classic lines was, "Begin with the end in mind." To make our vision a reality, Covey asked us to imagine the finished product before we begin to create a plan. With that finished product in mind, we return to the present moment and create and define measurable steps for a process that will lead us to the realization of our desired goal.

Though we do need a plan, we don't always know what the end result will be. God is often up to things far beyond our planning.

To finish well requires that we make adjustments now for a strong finish later. This way of planning for a strong finish has us start with the beginning—not the end—in mind. Before drafting a new set of life-plans, we will need to recapture the simplicity of our beginning if we are going to experience fruitfulness in our ending. This recaptured beginning will lay the groundwork for a fruitful finish.

THE PURPOSE OF FEELING STUCK

In a time of significant transition in my life, I read Terry Walling's book *Stuck!: Navigating Life and Leadership Transitions*. Jan actually read the book first and then handed her copy to me and said, "Read this. It explains a lot." I was drawn to Terry's book because it gave me permission to struggle with my emotions in times of reset and transition.

At the time, Jan and I sensed a change was taking place in our lives that would involve a new season and a new assignment. We were being prepared for this but did not have all the details. We were being made ready to break camp with a settlement we had known for a long time to venture forth and scout out new terrain— becoming pioneers once again. That preparation was emotionally challenging.

Terry informed his readers that just before a season

of significant change, we might become restless. Emotions will surface, and though they may seem concerning, they may also be a work of God. Our issues need to surface so that we can deal with them before entering the transition. What manifests as frustration and restlessness can often be personal opposition to what we have not yet entertained or considered as permissible.

Our emotions are gifts given from God. What we do with them is important. To let our emotions run free without examination and proper placement is to create roadblocks and diversions to our destination.

THE NEED FOR DISPERSAL

From the Day of Pentecost in Acts 2 through chapter 8 was a period of three to four years. The whole Book of Acts is not a day-by-day account of the Church. It spans decades. A lot of life took place between chapters.

After the Day of Pentecost, the Church began to gather around Solomon's Colonnade in the temple complex. This gathering place was the focal point of their lives between Acts 2 and 8. This is where they shared resources and life experiences, the place where signs and wonders and miracles happened with regularity.

During this time, people were forming community around the presence of God. As wonderful as all that was, something was missing. The Church was growing daily from its point of inception, but it was not moving beyond Jerusalem to engage the people and cultures of Judea, Samaria, and the uttermost parts of the Earth.

As people of faith—from the very beginning of our recorded history—we have loved to gather and stay gathered. Community is healthy and necessary. But it is unhealthy if it stalls the assignment given to us by Jesus—the assignment known as the Great

Commission. We have been given a mandate to tell the nations of the wonderful things God has done for humanity. We have also been called to leave our personal Jerusalem to venture outward with the Good News.

Our calling is one of expansion and exploration. This can be a physical or mental migration. Geographical expansion can come about through persecution, like the Early Church experienced or like the pilgrims who fled religious persecution in Europe to start a new life in America.

We can also expand by a change in thinking—in how we see our role in God's Kingdom. This often begins with feeling frustrated about the static status quo. We may glimpse a new and unrealized aspect of God and His Kingdom, and that insight will begin to stir the beginnings of a personal transition.

Expansion has been part of the spiritual DNA of the Church since Pentecost.

BREACHING REALMS

I recently watched a video of whales breaching the realm of water into the realm of air. On reaching the apex of their breach, the whales returned to the ocean, splashing back into their watery world to continue their journey of migration.

The film showed the action in slow motion, allowing the viewer to better see the details of the majestic breaching. In that slow-motion segment, I wondered what the whale might be thinking as he entered the realm of air and then re-submerged.

Immediately, I thought of how we live a life of faith. By an act of faith, we breach Heaven's realm and get a momentary glimpse into what was previously invisible, and we then return to our earthly environment. On our return, we splash back into what is known and begin to align our lives with what was seen for the first time in the breaching. This is where vision is cast.

Once we see beyond our familiar realm, we will bring back a passion to explore a new path because we saw something. We saw a new horizon, like a scout seeing new terrain.

C. S. Lewis coined the phrase, "baptized imagination," to describe what happened to his imagination after he became a follower of Jesus. He began to see the world differently through the lens of God's Spirit. His worldview was reordered by an immersion in a Spirit-empowered imagination. He caught a glimpse of things not yet seen in the earthly realm. This is where all great ideas in industry, government, and missions began.

Albert Einstein famously said:

> *Imagination is more important than knowledge. For knowledge is limited to all we now know and understand, while imagination embraces the entire world, and all there ever will be to know and understand.*

Imagination empowers the breaching of realms. It helps us see past mere details into the mind of Christ. Imagination takes us beyond what our current knowledge base defines as reality and helps us see the substance of things not yet considered by those chained to knowledge alone. Every great Kingdom endeavor began with someone who experienced a Spirit-empowered moment of imagination and considered for the first time something beyond the horizon line of existing knowledge.

Paul breached the limits of Earth's realm and soared into the realm of Heaven. He describes his experience:

"I was caught up to paradise and heard things so astounding that they cannot be expressed in words, things no human is allowed to tell" (II Corinthians 12:4

NLT).

The purpose of spiritual breaching is to give us a revelation of God. To know Him and to see from His perspective is the beginning of every endeavor of spiritual exploration and Kingdom expansion.

LIVING WITH EXPECTANCY

Imagine how our lives would change if we knew that barriers could be breached at any moment. I have noticed that when we expect the mercies of God and when we say *yes* to Him, He brings to light His deepest wonders. He unveils mysteries that were previously kept hidden (Jeremiah 33:3). When we experience a spiritual breakthrough as a result of these revelations, we become more open and willing to explore the territory of new ideas.

Embracing this expectant lifestyle will keep us looking toward Heaven, realizing that something more exists—something that often cannot be expressed in words. My desire is that you will breach the surface of something you cannot yet put in words, but which you know is there. It is something you feel in your heart that exists outside your current line of sight.

THE GREATEST SCOUT

Everything of value in this life comes when we discover something new about God and align our life with His heart and His plans. Long ago, He placed these good things on our timeline. He is excited for us to discover them; they reveal that He has gone before us into the future.

God is our Great Scout—our Way-Maker. We will never explore a place or have an experience that is unknown to Him. A new level of courage and commitment is birthed in us in that realization. Our trust is deepened each time we say *yes* to Him and follow His lead.

God begins each new journey by shifting the way we think. This is not always comfortable. It might look like severing unhealthy relationships, changing jobs, or moving to a new city or country. No matter what barrier we face, in Christ, we always carry what we need to breach the barriers inherent in the realm of our current way of thinking. Jesus makes these breaches with us, sharing the joy of our discovery.

I want to look more closely at the process of a thought-shift I experienced that realigned my focus and uncovered a passion I did not know existed. When the shift took place, I experienced a new alignment and found treasures buried in the path of my journey. God then used those sudden and unexpected discoveries to accelerate His purposes in me. Some of them took me by surprise.

DEFINING TIME

We use the word "suddenly" to describe unexpected experiences. In the Spirit, these can be like landmines of revelation, exploding and revealing something we had never considered or imagined. The appearance of these sudden breakthroughs has the power to strategically change our direction and the outcome of our efforts.

Two Greek words help us understand these sudden encounters with God. *Chronos* describes the unfolding of time in a linear and progressive fashion. From this word, we get our English word chronological; one event happens after another in a predictable direction. This is where human logic thrives. As we contemplate our future, our progress is often limited because *chronos* doesn't really require faith. It does not take discernment to understand a *chronos* measurement of time.

The Greek word *kairos* describes time that interrupts

the unfolding *chronos* timeline. God introduces a sudden and unexpected event into the chronology of our lives as He brings Heaven to Earth. Miracles happen in *kairos* time. So does the discovery of new technologies, insight for healthy cultural change, and spiritual breakthrough to heal old wounds.

Without the possibility of *kairos* moments, we will lack an important ingredient for a life of faith: wonder. As we explore the expanding edge of something new, driven by the wonder of what surrounds us, we are expectant. With Jesus, no matter what barrier we face, we always carry what we need to breach the realm of our current thinking. He makes these breaches with us, sharing the joy of our discovery.

When we return to Earth's realm, we know the stage has been set for the release of a *kairos* moment. That fresh word from God will be what fills us and holds us together when we return and face the nitty-gritty, life-threatening obstacles of this life.

The first-century spiritual explorers constantly made adjustments to the compass heading of their life mission in order to more precisely align their path with the Spirit's direction. Because of their obedience, everything changed, and God brought them unforeseen access points into culture, needed connections with strategic people, and a deeper understanding of His heart.

Like a child on Christmas morning who unwraps a brightly-wrapped present, these explorers were filled with a child-like wonder. This sense of wonder created a desire to exercise even more faith, inviting even more wonder as God moved on their behalf. Their encounters with God sustained them through great hardships, persecution, and martyrdom.

UNEXPECTED PARTNERSHIPS

In the Church, we have talked about new wineskins for

decades. These wineskins are not just another way to do the same thing. A new wineskin is not a new model for doing business, a new theological idea, or a new place to hold a church meeting. It is a new heart resulting in a renewed mind and a return to our first Love. Once we taste this new wine, new acts of inspired creativity will follow.

When Jesus spoke about new wineskins, nowhere in the text did he refer to a wineskin as a new model of anything (Luke 5). A new wineskin is a softened and moldable heart. From our renewed and refreshed heart will come new ways of living a life of faith.

When Jesus looked over the city of Jerusalem, the shortest verse in the Bible tells us, "Jesus wept." He wept because he realized the people did not yet see what they needed to see in order to move into the fullness God had planned for them.

Our mission is not about revolution; it's about reformation—the reforming of our hearts to align with God. A reformed heart will reframe our thinking. Once the reforming and reframing takes place, we will be able to display the beauty and power of the life of Jesus in culture with increased effectiveness. At that point, we become a new wineskin able to create and release new models of ministry and industry that will change the course of human history.

THE LANGUAGE OF REVIVAL

Wallace Henley, a revival historian, shared an interesting note about the Welsh Revival of 1904-1905. Henley wrote:

> *The transformation was so profound and so personal that the mules pulling the coal out of Welsh mines had to be retrained. They only knew the foul curses by which the miners drove them. But the converted miners quit cursing, and even the animals had to*

learn a new language.[1]

God wants the evidence of His presence to break out of our meetings and move into the streets. We love to fill up what I call our three C's: conferences, coliseums, and churches. While it is wonderful to see and experience a full venue, it will do little to steer the course of culture toward a flourishing future if those experiences remain stand-alone events.

We will know we have broken out of the orbital pull of attending just another meeting when we see real and lasting change taking place in the institutions of culture. Whether it is from the depths of a coalmine, behind the closed doors of a backroom political deal, or around the table of a corporate board meeting, the sound of personal integrity and honor is expressed with the language of a different Kingdom.

The evidence of this kind of change will be so profound that those involved will have to learn a new way of speaking to conduct business. The old language will no longer work.

A VISION OF SPILLED WINE

In a time of prayer, I saw the image of a group of people walking down a city street, only to discover they were walking through puddles of freshly spilled wine. Their feet were soaked with the wine.

As they moved through these roadways of culture, I could see that their hearts were broken. It did not appear to them that any new containers were available to collect the abundance of new wine that was continuing to spill onto the streets.

In the middle of their disappointment, the Lord told

[1] Wallace Henley. *Call Down the Lightning: What the Welsh Revival of 1904 Reveals About the Coming End Times.* Thomas Nelson. 2019.

them to ask Him for new wineskins. To contain and carry this new outpouring, He would give them strategies to produce new wineskins.

Then I saw this group walk through the doors of a church—leaving a trail of red, wine-stained footprints.

The next thing I saw was the arrival of new containers. No longer disappointed, this group was now able to collect and serve the new wine effectively to the people around them.

The new wine is the life of Jesus Christ in us. You and I are the wineskins. Only new containers that are soft and pliable have the capacity to hold the expanding qualities of new wine (Luke 5:37-38). Only a humble and softened heart can contain it.

We are in a *kairos* move of God. Holy-Spirit-led cultural reformers have entered into new spiritual territory. They will bring back the evidence of the new wine of the Spirit spilling out into the highways and by-ways of culture. On their return, they will extend an invitation to the Church to join them in this new venture.

Exploration is messy. Expansion upsets the norms of comfortable traditions. Historically, this desire to explore, discover, and partner with a new move of God is often unwelcomed by those who are in control of the status quo. An invitation to break camp with the status quo will at first appear disruptive and challenging. We cannot be defensive in these moments of challenge. Humility will be the pen that crafts the message of our invitation.

Jesus spoke of the quality of this new wine:

But new wine must be put into fresh wineskins.
And no one after drinking old wine desires new
wine, but says, "The old is good." (Luke 5:38-39 NRSV).

If we are going to be effective in a reforming effort,

we must speak with humility and honor. In order to be heard by certain segments within the Church, an explorer / reformer needs a heart of humility.

We can only give out what we personally have received from God. The quality of a pliable, humble heart is forged on the unmarked trails of life, where we move from self-assurance to a dependence upon Him.

I've learned the hard way how important a soft heart is. I have learned that whenever I am exposed to the harsh elements of my personal brokenness, I can expand my capacity to see my need for God's mercy. When this happens, I am better able to receive His grace and forgiveness. It is a humbling experience to be a new wineskin in the loving hands of God.

CHAPTER 4: SCOUTS—THE WAY-MAKERS

Scout: One sent to obtain information[1]

If scouts obtain information to lead those who will follow, it is vital that they accurately represent the destination. The journey must be worthwhile.

I met Dr. Dave Yarnes at a conference in Bend, Oregon. We were on a speaking roster along with several others. Dave is a self-described serial entrepreneur. He works as an executive coach and consultant in the field of business.

At the end of the conference, Dave handed me a copy of his book, *An Introduction to the Three Circle Strategy for a Fulfilling Life*. I began reading it after the conference.

Just a few pages in, Dave shared a powerful life experience. He had been waiting at the Washington Reagan Airport, engrossed in a conversation with his good friend, James Cannon. James asked a significant question that would change everything for Dave.

James is known as a wise businessperson who is philanthropic with his success. At the time, Dave was just beginning his own philanthropic endeavors. He valued counsel from a trusted mentor.

The conversation centered around the orphanages Dave and James had financially underwritten in East

---

[1] "scout." *Merriam-Webster Dictionary.* 2020. Web. 7 February 2020.

Africa in places of tremendous need. They spoke of lessons learned. They recalled the children from the orphanages who grew up to lead fulfilling and flourishing lives. It was a shared testimony of God's goodness.

Dave told James how, as a young father with a family, he was being pulled in so many directions and wanted to make sure he was focusing his efforts wisely. James stared at Dave intently, looked down at his watch, and then he looked at the boarding pass he was holding for his flight. He said he had to go but felt there was something he wanted to tell Dave that might not yet be obvious to him.

James said:

> *"You are at a crossroads, and it seems as if you are trying to go in a lot of directions, but there is really one question to be asked, and you're the only one that can answer it. Once you do, you will be able to focus your energy on making it a reality. Then every other aspect will fall in place naturally. When all is said and done, what will you have considered a worthy life?"*[3]

After James finished his comment, he stood, picked up his bag, said goodbye, and walked away to catch his flight.

When I finished reading about that encounter, I set Dave's book down and contemplated the profound nature of what I just read. The words "worth," "worthy," and "worthiness" became a template, overlaying the plan of my own life and helping me see where I might make any needed adjustments. I asked myself: Had I lived a worthy life? Had I discovered a destination worthy enough to invite

[3] Dave Yarnes. *An Introduction to the Three Circle Strategy for a Fulfilling Life.* Destiny Image. 2017. 20.

others to make a similar journey with me?

A worthy life is lived by someone who has discovered the essence of true worth. This is not the worth found in accomplishments or the wealth a person builds for oneself. It is something deeper—something only our Creator can reveal to each of us. It is a worth that comes from knowing we are loved by God and, because of that love, we can love others beyond ourselves.

A wise mentor, Jerry Cook, once shared, "Love is seeking the highest good for another person." Love defines worth. Value is a byproduct of love. A human without a sense of value will feel worthless and adrift.

There is so much we can follow in this life that has no lasting worth. So many things just promote self and self-interests and do nothing to advance God's Kingdom. We want to be people who are leading others to worthy destinations.

Worth protects us and guides us to right places and relationships and keeps us safe when something good can become the enemy of the best.

CHASING AFTER THE WIND

Nine times in the first six chapters of Ecclesiastes, Solomon uses the phrase "chasing after the wind." Life can become an ill-fated chase because we can pursue things and experiences that have no lasting meaning and are not aligned with a greater purpose. Solomon implies that to chase after even the good things in life without a greater purpose is a worthless chasing after the wind.

We would be wise to discover that higher purpose—a worthy destination—as soon as possible. Then, we will be able to build up and leave behind a testimony of meaning and substance.

INQUIRE OF THE LORD

Perhaps one of the greatest challenges in becoming a trustworthy scout is our ability to hear and discern the voice of the Lord. Many times, I have followed something that looked and sounded good, but upon closer examination, found it to be shallow, false, and worthless.

In my book, *The Leadership Rock,* I told a story about a pivotal time in my life. When Jan and I were based in Berlin, Germany, our assignment had us traveling quite a lot. Most weeks we found ourselves traveling by plane or train to a different European nation. On these trips, we met wonderful people in many diverse cultural settings.

On one such trip, I had finished teaching, and the meeting was coming to a close. A young man walked up to me. In a nervous voice, he said, "I think I have a word for you." He went on to share that giving prophetic words was something new and strange to him, but he wanted to be obedient. He told me the story of the Gibeonite deception found in the book of Joshua. His word was to remind me that I should always inquire of the Lord. After the meeting, I went to the Scripture to review the details surrounding that event.

Joshua 9 tells the story of the Gibeonites, the next-door neighbors to Jericho and Ai. They heard how Joshua and Israel had defeated Jericho and Ai, and they did not want to be next in line for a devastating defeat. So, they set up a ruse to get the Israelites to believe they had come from a distant land and they were not from the nearby nations Israel was planning to engage in battle.

But when the people of Gibeon heard what Joshua had done to Jericho and Ai, they resorted to deception to save themselves. They sent ambassadors to Joshua, loading their donkeys with weathered saddlebags and old, patched wineskins. They put on worn out, patched sandals and ragged clothes. And the bread they took with them was dry and moldy. When they arrived at the camp of Israel at Gilgal, they told Joshua and the men of Israel, "We have come from a distant land to ask you to make a peace treaty with us" (Joshua 9:3-6 NLT).

After hearing the Gibeonite's story, Israel made a terrible mistake:

So, the Israelites examined their food, but they did not consult the LORD. Then Joshua made a peace treaty with them and guaranteed their safety, and the leaders of the community ratified their agreement with a binding oath (Joshua 9:14-15).

Israel looked at the natural evidence the Gibeonites presented, but they did not inquire of the Lord. As a result, they bound themselves to an agreement that would forever require Israel to come to the defense of the Gibeonites. Yet they were supposed to be one of the conquered nations as Israel took possession of the Promised Land. Israel's agreement with them would become a visible scar on their nation and the leadership of Joshua.

Jan and I took this warning seriously. Warnings are precious gifts. Although we were in the habit of inquiring and not just assuming, the fact that God chose to specifically remind us gave an even stronger incentive to be on the alert.

The word from the young man was a gift for more than just that current season. Unknown to us, we were entering a time where we would make significant life decisions and enter a larger transition than we first thought. We needed wisdom and understanding when considering creating alliances with groups and individuals.

At every turn, we inquired of the Lord and then experienced His amazing grace. The passage in Joshua became a reminder of God's promise and provision. We might get shaken, but because we inquired of the Lord every time, we had confidence in His protection and peace. We will always be grateful for the word the young man had the courage to deliver.

God wants us to inquire of Him before we seek direction for our life and the lives of others. Many have explored unworthy destinations that have led to personal and corporate peril. In our scouting ventures, we will be presented with many options, and some will be like a Gibeonite deception. People will look, talk, and relate to us in what appears to be a right response, but just one query of the Lord could reveal something beneath the surface that would save us from making a disastrous decision.

RELATIONAL OR TRANSACTIONAL

Mark Simon is a good friend of mine. Mark and his wife, Margie, conduct strategic operation plans for individuals, corporations, faith movements, and organizations in every sphere of culture. The work Mark and Margie do is in-depth, professional, and life-changing.

On a visit to our home some years ago, Mark shared an interesting perspective that continually helps me keep my scouting ventures clear and free from dangerous assumptions and unhealthy alliances.

Mark told us his stories of success as well as loss. In the ups and downs of life, he discovered a God-given approach to living, whether it was a new friendship or forming an alliance for a business proposition.

He said that there are two ways to enter these relationships—transactional or relational. A transactional relationship, no matter how promising, is concerned only with the bottom line, the product created, and the profit gained. Personal integrity and honor can be easily pushed aside by the need to transact the deal at all costs, even the loss of relationship.

A relational partnership is based on honor and seeking the highest good for all involved. Mark no longer wanted to form transactional alliances without relationship. He wanted to be very intentional to first inquire of the Lord and not look only at surface values.

Like the Israelites, we can make decisions based on natural wisdom and outward appearance, only to discover we have been saddled with something we have no grace to handle. As with the Gibeonites, such ventures can become a burden.

God will build safeguards in our partnerships that we will discover when we ask Him for the right relationship and plan. If we move away from a relational environment toward a transactional methodology, no matter how successful the venture might appear on the surface, the foundation will not be solid and enduring. It can lose the more profound and long-lasting impact hoped for. Profit can't be our bottom line.

This way of thinking is foreign if we are only looking at numbers and outcomes or when we are motivated by selfish ambition and jealously. Quite possibly, the next great breakthrough in any field will come when our relationships have been reformed by honor, not profit.

Whether a trail traveled during the exploration of the American West or a modern-day development of a new technology, these journeys are filled with conflict, barriers, and danger. Teams need to be committed to each other even more than to their shared assignment. We want to survive the journey and arrive at a place of fulfillment intact—spiritually and emotionally. Honor and shared loyalty are paramount to the success of any venture.

God can do more with love, honor, and loyalty than with the most gifted team whose motives do not reflect the values of God's Kingdom.

INQUIRING OF GOD FOR DIVINE STRATEGIES

For years, I have been hiking the trails above our home. One day I noticed that the trail management had posted a new sign that read: "Not a Designated Trail." I felt that the sign was a metaphor for something the Lord wanted to say.

Some of the familiar paths we have walked in the past will no longer lead us to our God-ordained future. These trails have been marked by the Lord as, "Not a Designated Trail." We can no longer follow assumptions from the past. It is important to inquire of the Lord at every fork in the trail and to follow the signs He places on our paths. For some of us, it means returning to the trailhead of a previous discovery and reviewing the original map of our calling. In that review, we will see a corrected destination and receive a resulting redirection.

Perhaps the greatest of Old Testament leaders was David. Even though David had his flaws, God called him a man after His own heart. I think one reason for this description was David's willingness to inquire of God before making decisions. One such incident is recorded in II Samuel 5: 17-25, when he asked an important question, "Should I...?"

> When the Philistines heard that David had been anointed king of Israel, they mobilized all their forces to capture him. But David was told they were coming, so he went into the stronghold. The Philistines arrived and spread out across the valley of Rephaim. So David asked the Lord, "Should I go out to fight the Philistines? Will you hand them over

to me?" The Lord replied to David, "Yes, go ahead. I will certainly hand them over to you" (NLT).

Life is filled with decisions. Like David, someday you may face an enemy who is determined to wipe you off the face of the earth—probably more figuratively than literally. You will have to make a life-and-death decision. If you have a heart after God, you will always ask Him, "Should I do this?"

There are perilous issues waiting on the future paths of hasty decisions made without inquiring of the Lord. These decisions can bring unnecessary pain and sorrow. Those situations can be avoided if we inquire of the Lord and don't make hasty assumptions.

David's victories were not accomplished with his strength and wisdom. The text continues in verse 20:

> *So David went to Baal-perazim and defeated the Philistines there. "The Lord did it!" David exclaimed. "He burst through my enemies like a raging flood!" So, he named that place Baal-perazim (which means the Lord who bursts through).*

Because David relied on God's strategy and partnered with Him, The Breaker of Heaven entered the battle, giving David an anointing to break through to win the battle.

Inquiry is not a one-time event. Some battles will require multiple inquiries of the Lord. This is not a day-by-day inquiry. It is a moment-by-moment inquiring. We may move past one barrier in a project or mission only to encounter another obstacle from the same source. The insight we received from God for a past battle may not be what brings victory in a future battle.

The words "and again" jumped out of the text at me when I read these next verses.

> But after a while the Philistines returned and again
> spread out across the valley of Rephaim. And again
> David asked the Lord what to do. "Do not attack
> them straight on," the Lord replied. "Instead, circle
> around behind and attack them near the poplar trees.
> When you hear a sound like marching feet in the
> tops of the poplar trees, be on the alert! That will be
> the signal that the Lord is moving ahead of you to
> strike down the Philistine army." So David did what
> the Lord commanded, and he struck down the
> Philistines all the way from Gibeon to Gezer (II
> Samuel 5: 22-25).

David again asked the Lord for His marching
orders. He inquired. He did not assume. This battle
required an entirely different approach. Assumption
would have placed David and his army in the wrong
position to experience victory.

I respect sound business practices, collegial
relationships, and proven ways of getting things done.
I can be impressed with knowledgeable, confident-
sounding counsel. What I respect most is someone who
will say, "Let's ask the Lord, again." This takes guts,
especially when a plan is in place ready to execute, and
a delay could incur added costs and disappointment
for those who backed the project.

I want to have a heart after God and a track record
of inquiring of Him no matter the cost. I want to
position my life and my team in a place where God is
able to burst through the lines of opposition and bring
unusual victory.

IN QUIETNESS AND TRUST

Advance, accelerate, and breakthrough are not always
the way forward. In your spiritual gut, you will know
when your assignment is to retreat into an isolated
place with God. This retreat might make no sense, to

you or to those who work with you. But if you hear a word of the Lord, follow His instruction. The very thing you need to discover to move forward through strident opposition will not be found in forward progress. It will be found by retreating into the heart of God.

As the prophet Isaiah said, "In quietness and trust is your strength" (30:15 NIV). Retreat to that quiet place, and you will be refreshed and empowered. From that place of rest, new revelation awaits.

UNSEEN PATHWAYS

I was processing a verse in the Psalms: "Your road led through the sea, your pathway through the mighty waters—a pathway no one knew was there!" (Psalm 77:19 NLT). The last part of the verse struck a deep chord in my soul, "a pathway no one knew was there."

Parting the Red Sea is not an isolated event in history. If you are emotionally or spiritually standing at the end of the road and no longer see a possible way ahead, decree God's Word over your circumstance. The simple act of declaring His truth is to come into agreement with Heaven.

We serve a God who delights in revealing roads of hope no one knew were there. He wants to reveal such pathways to you.

UNDERSTANDING PACE

The early frontier scouts were not leading people on a paved highway. They moved through vast stretches of wilderness without trails or road signs. They made decisions on the move, keeping in mind those who would someday be following and the speed at which they would travel.

Pioneers traveled the Applegate Trail in wagons pulled by oxen. A team of oxen could only move about two miles per hour, and that was on flat ground with no obstacles. Wagons could not traverse a mountain like a man on horseback. If a top-heavy wagon tried to make a trail around a mountain, it would tip over. Instead, a wagon had to traverse mountains head-on—straight up the incline in order to remain upright. Many times, this meant using several teams of oxen hitched together to get each wagon up and over an intimidating mountain range.

This kind of work took time and patience. On the other side of a steep grade, the pioneers would reverse the process and guide each wagon down the slope, held in check by a rope tied to men and teams of oxen. This was done one wagon at a time, until all the wagons reached flat ground. An entire day could be spent getting all the wagons up a steep grade, and then the entire next day would be spent lowering the wagons down to the valley below. This made for really slow progress, sometimes less than a mile in a single day.

A wise scout needs to pick a route knowing the limitations of those who will follow. Scouts must consider the time-consuming and energy-draining obstacles pioneers will face.

PLURAL PLANS

God has more than one plan for each life, and He can make each one work no matter what kind of derailment has taken place. During a lunch conversation with my daughter, Anna, she mentioned the plural usage of the word "plans" in Jeremiah 29:11:

> For I know the plans I have for you, says the Lord. They are plans for good and not for disaster, to give you a future and a hope (NLT).

I looked up the verse to read it again with fresh

eyes. I realized the beauty of God's creative ability when it comes to our failed plans. He is the infinite God of all things, including a new plan when our original plan failed.

If a plan does not work out, other plans are not less valuable than the original plan.

God is waiting to redirect people whose plans were painfully dismantled. He wants us to believe He has more goodness in store for us beyond the pain of what fell apart.

SPEAKING IN TWO VOICES

Scouts speak with two voices: the apostolic voice and prophetic voice.

The apostolic voice sees and maps out a trail to a new destination. Throughout the journey, the apostolic voice helps the group maintain mission integrity and stay focused on the larger blueprint of the endeavor.

A scout will also speak a prophetic word of hope at just the right moment to encourage weary travelers. Scouts encourage pioneers to stay focused on God's word and to stand on His promise, regardless of the circumstances. They warn against taking shortcuts that will jeopardize a favorable outcome.

These two functions are critical for any journey. You might be entering new territory, crossing a new threshold, or engaging a new assignment, traveling a new way you have never been before.

There will likely be pushback and opposition to the new way because the territory you are entering has never been breached before. In those moments, stand on the original word the Lord revealed. His word will never fail to return without an increase.

Nothing God says is void of supernatural potential when captured and exercised by faith.

TRANSPORTED BY LOVE

One day, while stopped at a traffic light, I began to hear the bleating of a lamb. I thought it was something on my radio. Then I heard it again. I looked to my left and realized a lamb was inside a custom-made transport crate, securely held in the bed of a pickup truck. I could tell the person driving the truck cared about the lamb by the way he had prepared to transport the animal.

The lamb was bleating because it had no idea what was happening. It did not know this was all being done to make sure it would arrive safely at its new destination.

The lamb looked and sounded like someone who is being moved to a new and unfamiliar place. There are times when God will put us in the crate of an unusual expression of His love to keep us safe during the journey. When the journey begins, these crates make no sense to us. We want to go back to the familiar open pasture we knew where things made sense and life was predictable.

Before we label any transport as negative, we need to ask the Lord if this is something He is doing for our own welfare. When surrounded by so many unfamiliar things, we need to understand that He is trying to get us through the dangerous traffic of life to arrive safely at a new pasture. Such was the journey of the first pioneers, and such can be a reoccurring event anytime God moves us under His protective hand to a new destination.

SCOUTS HELP PIONEERS CROSS BOUNDARIES

Southern Oregon was one of the last regions of the Oregon Territory to be explored and mapped. The Siskiyou Mountains that straddle the border between

California and Oregon were once called the Boundary Mountains. These mountains marked the boundary between the Oregon Territory and Spanish California.

The early pioneers crossed many of these boundaries. Some were ancient and had been defined by indigenous people groups and mountain men. Other boundaries were lines drawn by political factions with agendas for future domination. A scout had to be aware of these boundaries and lead those in their trust through them without creating unnecessary conflict.

A present-day scout will cross numerous boundaries to gather intelligence. A contemporary venture must cross boundary lines of impossibility, relational restriction, legal challenge, or a lack of funding before it arrives at its final destination. This is where a scout must not compromise by taking a deadly shortcut that could lead to casualties.

In leadership theory, these passages are called boundary events. They mark boundaries that need to be wisely navigated in order to move forward. Embedded in these boundary events are integrity checks we must pass through; if we don't, the journey will stall in canyons of fear or dishonor.

Each new venture will be marked by these boundary events. As I have passed through the ones in my own life, I discovered that the condition of my heart comes before what I am tasked to do.

Once I navigate through a personal integrity check, I become aware of what needs to change in my heart. With a heart change, I have greater wisdom to see new possibilities.

SPIRITUAL CONTRACTORS

My dad was a contractor. He built houses, and before he could build a new house, he had to obtain a set of blueprints based on an architect's design. The blueprints were large, blue-inked pages of construction plans. Dad kept them rolled up and close at hand so that he and his construction team could make sure each stage of a building project remained true to its original design.

Dad also carried these plans with him in his pickup truck when he met with subcontractors or when he ordered building materials. I remember him walking out onto a vacant lot with his clients as he began to imagine where the house would sit on the land. He would talk with his clients while holding up an unfurled set of blueprints.

My dad was imagining what was about to be created. He was scouting a construction job site that would lead to the creation of a new home for a family. The clients trusted his interpretation of the blueprints that would someday lead them across the threshold of their new home.

Following a scout is about trust. My dad's clients trusted him to create a new home on a vacant lot. They entrusted him with their ideas and dreams.

TRUSTING AND BEING TRUSTED

In the summer of 1846, Jesse Applegate and Levi Scott needed to persuade the pioneers to overcome their fear and reluctance in order to follow them on a new trail.

Most of the Applegate Trail pioneers walked the 2,000 miles of their westward journey. The early pioneers had a lot of jeopardy to overcome, not only from the elements, terrain, and hostile encounters, but also from the drain on their emotions and physical strength. Their life-altering decision to travel westward hinged on a scout's promise to lead them safely to their destination.

The same is true today when we are moving in a shift age of rapid advancement into new places of discovery. Scouts explore the expanding edge of a fresh revelation. God gives them an apostolic blueprint, which provides a destination. The prophetic voice of a scout offers the sound of hope that keeps the pioneers advancing toward the outcome of an apostolic blueprint.

RIGHTEOUS PERSUASION

A scout will ask a critical question of themselves before a journey begins: Do I have a word from God? God's word carries an authority to overcome obstacles and empower weary travelers. You may appear uneducated and rough, or you may be a gifted, influential leader. Regardless, you want His authority and anointing to be able to communicate with confidence and clarity that a new way is possible. That requires a word from God.

If you are persuading a group to follow you, craft your message and present it with confidence that only comes from inquiring and hearing from God. He will empower you to share what your listeners will need to hear. He will protect you and guide you through the unknown circumstances you did not foresee if you remain true to His word.

Investors and subsequent followers do not care much for bravado when their lives, the wellbeing of their families, and their resources are on the line. When a scout meets potential pioneers, the proposal they extend as an invitation needs to speak to the heart as well as the head. Once the heart is convinced, the head will follow.

BELONGING BEFORE BELIEVING

I have always thought it remarkable that Jesus would allow twelve, untested men who follow Him to conduct the most powerful spiritual interactions. The twelve were not yet believers in a traditional sense.

They were not filled with the Spirit—that would take place later as recorded in John 20.

These disciples, and later the 70, would be given authority to heal the sick, cast out demons, and participate in miracles—all before they fit neatly into our definition of a new-covenant disciple. Jesus had a level of trust not often seen in the Church today. A scout will need to develop the same heart as Jesus.

Imagine a strong and experienced scout leading a group of individuals who probably had never seen a wilderness, let alone tried to survive in its challenging environment. Most of what they needed to learn would be acquired on the journey.

These were trying experiences, emotionally and physically. An impatient scout could quickly demoralize a wagon train full of first-time pioneers if they focused on their inexperience and insecurity.

If you are the one responsible for choosing the scout for your group, be careful who you choose to represent your vision. Make sure they agree with your mission and heart. They will set the first impressions representing you, your concept, and mission. Choosing the wrong scout can be a fatal mistake for those who follow their lead.

ACTIONABLE INTELLIGENCE

Recently, I was listening to an interview of a Navy SEAL team leader describing a successful operation. The SEAL team had been tasked with the rescue of a downed pilot. After capturing an enemy combatant and completing a detailed interrogation, the team was able to gather enough actionable intelligence to plan a rescue and get the pilot out of enemy territory alive.

Actionable intelligence is information that has enough substance and verification to reduce risk to the rescue team and increase the probability of a successful outcome for the operation.

As I considered the words "actionable intelligence," I thought about the correlation to exploration. We need detailed, actionable, prophetic intelligence to move into something new—without just repeating the past. Business plans, ministry endeavors, and personal life decisions will require distinct and actionable intelligence unique to our current circumstance.

God is ready and waiting to uncover and divulge the perfect plan needed to step over the limitations of our life-experience. He loves sharing His actionable and measurable steps, making them available to all who are willing to hear what assumption and a pre-determined outcome cannot provide. The prophet Amos said: "Indeed, the Sovereign Lord never does anything until he reveals his plans to his servants the prophets" (Amos 3:7-8 NLT).

Some scouts will wonder why they are considered for an assignment, especially if they do not have the expected background or acumen in a particular sphere of influence. There are times when the way forward is not discovered with existing knowledge of a technology or a political ideology. It is discovered by revealing the heart of God at a critical juncture.

I am part of several groups where I know nothing of the industry, technology, or governmental procedures being considered. Critical moments of advancement do not necessarily come from learning more about the product or issues they want to develop.

In these groups, I can be someone who intervenes on people's behalf by inquiring of the Lord. What He unveils to me might affect the relational makeup of a team and their cohesiveness, helping them to advance. He might give a warning, a matter of timing, or a fresh insight in order to see the road ahead more clearly. We are all called to represent the heart of God, which in the end, is always the way forward.

Actionable prophecy will require courage, just like

it required courage for Noah to announce a coming flood that no one believed possible. He was mocked until it started to rain.

Actionable, prophetic insight will reveal the source of embedded deceptions expressed in unhealthy models of authority, and entrenched power structures.

Unlikely prophetic voices are being positioned by God in all spheres of influence. In these placements, God's power will be expressed for all to see. No human prediction or expertise could have revealed the details these words will deliver.

THE HONOR BOX

For the last 20 years, I have driven past a small sign on a country road near my home advertising homemade jams and jellies. One day, I decided to turn around and check it out.

Just off the main road, at the end of a dirt driveway sat a small, wooden table. When I got out of my car to inspect the articles for sale, I found jars of pumpkin butter and jams and jellies made of apricot or berries. Each jar was decorated with a tiny bow.

On the table sat a handwritten note listing the cost of the items. What caught my attention was a small box with a slot where I could deposit my money. No one was in sight. I bought several jars and dropped a twenty in the box. I named it the "Honor Box."

Every transaction in life has an honor box somewhere. While I had no thought to rob anyone, including this person who made jam, there are other areas in my life where passing the honor-box test is a challenge.

I need the conviction and warnings of God's Spirit concerning my heart issues—whether unbelief, wrong thinking, or a negative response to life. I continually invite God to renew my mind so that I can be sensitive to His voice. God has already completed the plan for me to be able to finish well. It will be up to me to keep saying *yes* to Him at each step.

All of us need these integrity checks to our character. We all have honor boxes lining our path. Many are not recognizable by us or others—only by God. They can resemble an unguarded jam and jelly stand, an expense account, or a second look at a forbidden image. We will make a deposit before we move on. Those deposits—or the lack of them—will direct the course of our lives.

A PARROT, A PUPPET, OR A PROPHET

Scouts have three choices that will determine the impact, the quality, and the content of their voice. As prophetic scouts, we can function in our God-given gifts, or we can become a parrot or a puppet.

The parrots we see in cages are trained to repeat statements they hear without understanding the actual meaning or the source of what they are parroting. They simply repeat a script.

Puppets respond to life at the whim and control of their puppet masters, who dictate the message and the response to it. Puppets dance at the end of controlling strings held by people who have never ventured past the border of the status quo they desire to protect. The puppet masters want to protect this boundary at all costs, even to the loss of integrity. They view any consideration of expansion as a threat.

God is not a Puppet Master, and people are not His puppets. He is sovereign, and His word will be fulfilled. In His sovereignty, He has given us a will to choose or reject truth. If we want to partner with Him, we will have to learn to listen to His voice and desire to respond only to Him, both personally and in public. What will define the sound and content of our voice was written by Paul in Romans 8:5: "But those who live by the impulses of the Holy Spirit are motivated to pursue spiritual realities" (TPT).

Only by responding to the impulses and direction of God's Spirit can we discern truth and confidently proclaim that truth to others. It is critical to continually discern the difference between a tug on a puppet string or an impulse of His Spirit.

God raises up prophetic leaders who address deeply embedded cultural issues that parrots and puppets never see or consider. When you obey God, your voice and your actions will stand out—and in some cases stand alone—in a culture filled with the sight and sound of flailing puppets and noisy parrots.

A MESSAGE FROM THE WILDERNESS

At a pivotal point in human history, John the Baptist displayed great courage. He was announcing to the world that what had been foretold centuries before was now being fulfilled; the Messiah had come. John prophesied a new day with a new covenant had arrived (Matthew 3).

John told the people to repent for the Kingdom of God was at hand. He was calling out to the status quo of his day, announcing that change was approaching. It took courage because the message would shake the establishment and those who followed the limitations of that old paradigm. The new was replacing the old, and that new message would cost John his head.

CONFESSION & REPENTANCE FOR THE BETTER

The word repent means "to change one's mind." It is a shift in our thinking. In Matthew 3, where John challenged the people to repent, the word "repent" in that context also has three words added to its definition: to change one's mind *for the better*. Unless a scout can express a better way, people will be unwilling to leave their intellectual and spiritual encampments to follow something new—a better way, leading to a better place. The Scripture states: "People from Jerusalem and from all of Judea and all over the Jordan Valley went out to see and hear John (Matthew 3:5 NLT)." John's word of repentance shook the culture.

An act of repentance resulting in a change of mind must be preceded by a confession.

When we traditionally think of confession, we link it to sinful behavior. That is often true, but the original word means something more. To confess means to agree.

Before any change can take place in our thinking, and before we are willing to follow the intelligence and wisdom of the ultimate scout, Jesus, we need to confess—to be in agreement with Him.

The impetus to agree with Him is to know that He is leading us on a better pathway and to a better place. In order to do that, our beliefs, heart attitude, thinking, and behavior need to align in a mutual agreement with Him.

When we agree with what Jesus is saying about sin or about anything, we are saying *yes* to His assessment and way of thinking concerning His heart for us. He wants to fulfill our destiny with Him. He desires to give us all we were created for: to know Him and be known by Him.

My *yes* gives Him freedom to commune with me so that I can experience belonging and family. As my Father, He protects and provides for me. By His Spirit, He shows me the compassionate, nurturing love of a mother's heart. He is my elder brother, my closest confidant, my best Friend.

Can two walk together unless they are in agreement (Amos 3:3)? The power of our *yes* releases divine agreement with Heaven. We no longer operate independently from Jesus. We are now one with Him, carrying out His mission—which becomes our mission.

NOT ALL WILL FOLLOW

God might ask you to cut and paste a portion of an old vision into the new thing He is doing in you. I've found that His unfolding vision is sometimes similar to the process of writing a book.

By the time I begin a book, I usually have written content that previously stood alone and has been stored in separate files on my computer. This content might not have had a unifying context before the book idea comes, but when does, I can cut and paste that content into a new file and begin the larger writing project.

When I begin a new book, I am always glad I saved those past writings. In a similar way, it is not wise to prematurely hit the delete button on our past before we inquire of the Lord.

Some of the things in your history were not just to carry for a single season. They are part of your spiritual and visionary core and should migrate with you into the future. Vision is accumulated and crafted over a lifetime. It's not a static, one-time event created in an afternoon life-planning workshop.

With each new season, you will need to discern what is to remain with you and what you should leave behind.

In the summer of 1846 in Fort Hall, Idaho, not everyone who heard the invitation to travel the Applegate Trail accepted the proposal. Of the multiple hundreds of wagons assembled, only 100 wagons were willing to follow and become the trail's first pioneers.

Don't be thrown off task by a limited response when you first propose a new idea. You are forging a trail though unexplored wilderness. Not everyone is eager for such a journey. The first ones to follow your lead will become a living testimony of the wisdom and insight God gave you.

STAY IN YOUR LANE

After thirty-five years of pastoral ministry, Jan and I knew that an assignment had ended. We handed over the church we had been pastoring for fifteen years to the next generation. They were a well-seasoned leadership team, most of whom had been with us from the beginning. It was a joyful process watching God affirm the transition.

Before handing off the reins of leadership, I asked the Lord to show me what my life would look like in the next season. Immediately, I saw a very large room. It was a vast auditorium that felt empty. Then the Lord directed my attention to a small circular table in the middle of the room. The top of the table was illuminated, and on it sat three plates. Atop each plate was a single word: speak, write, and mentor.

At that moment, I knew the Kingdom assignment God had for me in the coming years. I was free to focus on speaking, writing, and mentoring. I was no longer tied to the daily demands of pastoring a local church and could focus with greater clarity on the three areas that were a passion for me. I had grace for these three assignments. It's important to not overstep what God is saying and directing but rather to "stay in my lane."

It has been several years since God gave me that clarification. He also gave me the ability to focus more precisely on those specific areas of calling, and it has been fulfilling in many ways.

Every new season has a new lane in which we are to travel. Before you enter the onramp for the next season, ask the Lord what lane you are to travel. It will make the journey more joy-filled and productive if you inquire of the Lord.

SCOUTING REPORTS

When Moses sent out twelve scouts into the Promised Land, only Joshua and Caleb came back with a positive report. Even among these handpicked leaders, not everyone saw the same thing. Ten scouts said they looked like grasshoppers in comparison to the obstacles that stood between them and the promise. Joshua and Caleb saw the same obstacles as the other scouts but interpreted what they saw through the lens of faith, not fear. Their spiritual character determined the quality of the intelligence they gathered.

Whenever God leads us into new territory, He will ask us to see what lies ahead with His eyes, not ours. He is asking us to see the substance of things not yet visible to the natural eye.

In Isaiah 43:19, the Lord describes this principle of sight: "For I am about to do something new. See, I have already begun! Do you not see it?" (NLT). Twice the word "see" is used in this passage; it means to perceive or to discern something rightly. It is a verb that describes action. It is something we must do in faith.

Whenever you step into a new venture, especially regarding a promise, things that stand in the way of your advancement will appear like giants. At that point, you have a choice to see them through the lens of human ability and intellect or to see them through the lens of God's word. The places with the greatest potential will always have the tallest giants guarding the unharvested promise.

May the light of God illuminate the eyes of your imagination, flooding you with light and giving you 20/20 vision, until you experience the full revelation of your great hope of glory—the substance of His presence. Explore and experience for yourself all the riches of this wealth freely given to you, for you are His true inheritance (Ephesians 1:18, my paraphrase).

FIVE QUESTIONS FOR A SCOUT

1) Are you leading people to a worthy destination?

Worth is not something you create; it is a God-given value. Worth is the by-product of love. To lead well, your assignment and destination need to be commissioned by God. Equally important, you must discover the worth of those you lead from God's perspective. This knowledge will help you define a worthy destination and give value to the intelligence you gather for setting the course of the journey. It will also determine how you treat others when, in moments of weakness and fear, they want to give up. You will encourage them forward with words of worth and worthiness—powerful motivators.

2) Have you inquired of the Lord?

Some detours could lead you to a place of peril and unnecessary expenditure of strength and resources. Filter every decision through a word from God. His truth leads you, not your assumptions. Assumptions create jeopardy and bondage. Inquire and He will answer.

3) Is the intelligence you gathered doable?

You can scout a route that is only passable by a skilled mountain climber, but in reality, not all who follow your lead can scale the shear rock face you ask them to climb. The way must be able to be navigated together, or you have not done your homework.

4) Do you understand righteous persuasion?

After you gather intelligence for the journey, you will need to recruit a group to follow you. Just laying out facts without the passion and sincerity that hope creates will not encourage people to risk life and limb to follow your lead. Righteous persuasion is far more than a good sales pitch. It is speaking the truth in love, from a sincere heart, committed to the wellbeing of prospective pioneers.

5) What voice will you use?

In the scouting phase, you will speak with two main voices: the apostolic and the prophetic. At points in your presentation—and all along the way—you will move back and forth between these two voices, depending on the needs that surface on the trail. The apostolic voice will reveal God's blueprint. The prophetic voice will release encouraging words to help people navigate the most daunting terrain.

There are times when vision is blurred from fatigue and conflict. At those moments, the apostolic gift will pull out the larger blueprint, stating why the journey was undertaken in the first place, keeping the team focused on the bigger picture.

Like Habakkuk, prophets steward God's plan. They understand the times and seasons (Habakkuk 2:2-3) and help pioneers keep moving under the impulse of God's Spirit.

A prophetic voice also functions as an intercessory guard, giving warnings that will protect the people from unnecessary harm. They intercede for the people, the chosen trail, and the eventual destination.

CHAPTER 5: PIONEERS—THE PROMISE-FOLLOWERS

Pioneer: a person who is one of the first people to do something.[1]

In the process of exploration, pioneers follow scouts. In the expansion of the American West, pioneers survived a challenging journey and arrived fatigued and threadbare to the place of their dreams. In reality, their journey was only just beginning on arrival. Another level of adaptability awaited them as they prepared to survive in a new territory.

Recently, I read an article about a new concept of Japanese elevators. These elevators can move in four different directions: not just up and down but also side to side. They can move a passenger chamber across a building and then up or down to access waiting passengers on any floor. This design adjusts to changing needs and dramatically cuts down wait time.

Such is the essence of a pioneering spirit. A pioneer learns to adjust to rapidly changing circumstances. They can move laterally as easily as linearly.

PERSONAL PIONEERING

In 1981, Jan and I sold our home in Springfield,

---

[1] "pioneer." *Cambridge Dictionary.* 2020. Web. 12 February 2020

Oregon. Jan packed our two kids and two cats into the Subaru, and I drove a large rental van containing all our earthly possessions. We headed out to Kalispell, Montana to plant a new church. This was our first attempt at pastoring. Those who sent us called us pioneer pastors.

On the way to Montana, we crossed the Columbia River near Umatilla, Oregon, and drove north toward the Tri-Cities in Washington. A few miles outside Umatilla, the highway was closed. A range fire was burning out of control, threatening those traveling on the highway. We had no choice but to turn around and grab a motel in Umatilla for the night. The next day, the fire had moved on and the road was clear.

I planned the trip from Oregon to Montana in great detail but did not plan for a range fire that would alter our plans. We were only focused on our destination. Our timing had changed, but not our destination. We had to adapt our plans. Pioneers must remain flexible and be able to encounter change and execute alternate plans when the unexpected crosses their path.

FACING OBSTACLES

Adaptability is at the core of a pioneering spirit. While the scouts of the American West surveyed and reported the best route to travel, they could not foresee the ever-changing, daily adjustments that would be required. This was the job of a pioneer. In many cases, a scout would be away from the wagon train for extended periods. He needed to make sure the trail ahead was clear and safe. In his absence, it was up to the pioneers to navigate under the management of a wagon master or an elected wagon train captain.

Progress was rarely a straight line for the wagon trains. The same is true for someone in the twenty-first century following a dream. Lateral motion and even course reversals to return to a missed juncture are part of the journey. Life is not always onward and upward.

DELAYED DEPARTURE

Every journey of exploration will involve some form of sorrow and pain. Something deep within us—the hope of a worthy destination—gives us a courage not realized in the comfort of the life we left behind. In the moments of our greatest challenge, God gives us an inner strength we did not previously possess. This grace-empowered gift of endurance is not something we create. It is a gift of grace that empowers us to press on and not give up.

As I've mentioned, when the first pioneers arrived at their intended destination, their original clothes and footwear had either worn away or rotted off. These pioneers did not look like cast members from *Little House on the Prairie*. Many had replaced their original clothing with articles fashioned from the skins of the animals they harvested as food on the journey.

In addition to the hardships they encountered on the trail, the Applegate wagon train of 1846 had gotten off to a late start from the beginning, putting them at greater risk for encountering winter storms. Sure enough, a storm rolled in from the Pacific, creating a life-and-death struggle for survival.

The same massive winter storm that created a cold, soaking rain along the northern route of the Applegate Trail, dumped multiple feet of snow in the winter of 1846-1847 in the Sierra Nevada Mountains of California. The other pioneers in the initial group of wagons who left from Fort Hall, Idaho, traveled west toward California. Tragically, they became known as the Donner Party.

One of the pioneers in the Applegate Wagon Train wrote in his diary of the problems the storm created as they pressed through a formidable canyon during the storm:

We started through on Monday morning and reached the opposite plain on Friday night after a series of breakdown, hardships and being constantly wet. Laboring hard and very little to eat. The provisions being exhausted in the whole company. We ate our last the evening we got through. Rain started to fall on October 26ᵗʰ and continued for five days.

The pioneers had been caught in the bottom of Canyon Creek just south of present-day Canyonville, Oregon. The canyon walls were almost vertical, and the creek was running at flood stage under the torrent of a winter storm. Fallen timber and boulders blocked their way. They had to make it through the canyon, or they would die.

One account described the wagon train like a retreating army, defeated in battle, off-loading the last of their supplies in retreat.

Seven people perished from hunger and exposure in the canyon. It took the survivors five days to travel the nine miles through the canyon, pulling and pushing wagons over and around fallen logs and large boulders. Some of these pioneers became so desperate, they even abandoned their wagons and completed the remainder of the journey on foot.

In his diary, Tolbert Carter wrote:

The Umpqua canyon was a terror to the company. The sides seemed almost perpendicular. It didn't seem possible for a wagon and team to get down it, but somehow they did.

᠎ Diary of Virgil K. Pringle, pioneer on the 1846 Applegate Trail.
᠎ Tolbert Carter. *Pioneer Days*. Transactions of the Oregon Pioneers Association, 1906.

"But somehow they did" is a reoccurring theme of pioneers in any Kingdom endeavor. Every journey has a canyon we must traverse if the purpose for our journey is to become a reality. The passage will either kill our dream or become a testimony of God's unfailing love. When we have nothing left to give, trust is our only remaining resource.

In the depths of that dire canyon experience, in a life and death struggle for survival, the broken pioneers were ready to give up and die. Pioneer Levi Scott wrote:

> ...and I must say a dreadful canyon, where we really could go no further without having made a road through this formidable gorge. I spent two days in a fruitless endeavor to get a party to go with me... Finally I emphatically called the company to attention, and told them that I was going through the next morning....If no one would go with me.....I should go home, "I will not stay, idly, here and see you all perish, because you will not put forth an effort to help yourself."[,]

He expressed the kind of leadership required not only when people are ready to give up and die but at any leg of the journey when the way forward seems impossibly blocked. A pioneering principle emerges in these experiences. We cannot help people move beyond the point where they are unwilling to step up and help themselves. At some point, they must move on or we will die.

It was in the worse moments that everything the

[,] From Levi Scott's recollections of personal notes titled "From Independence to Independence." Collected by the Hugo Neighborhood Association and Historical Society from their archives.

pioneers possessed was tested to the limit. Their resources were depleted, and their energy had long drained away. They were left in a cold place of exposure, facing impossible odds. Yet they chose to pick up their feet one at a time and continue beyond their personal limitations. They offloaded much of their belongings and kept moving in hopes of arriving alive in the Willamette Valley.

We will all encounter deep and dark canyons that challenge everything about ourselves and our calling— sometimes even to the point of mission failure. These critical moments when everything is on the line will require the kind of leader who will speak the unvarnished truth in love. We have the choice to sit down and die or to get up and keep moving toward the word of promise God has spoken.

A century after those pioneers crossed the canyon, it was filled in to create the roadbed for Interstate 5. Whenever I drive along that stretch of road, I become quiet and reflect on that very difficult moment of passage for my ancestors.

During the journey through Canyon Creek, my relative, Alfonso Boone, the grandson of Daniel Boone, had to bury some of his belongings in a cache. Among his belongings were Daniel Boone's compass and survey equipment. Alphonso would return a year later to retrieve his belongings, but the cache had been vandalized and the items stolen. I imagine what it would be like for someone to discover my uncle's compass and survey equipment.

I believe God sent our family to Oregon as a fulfillment of the prayers offered by my relatives and others on the first Applegate Wagon Train. Any loss they experienced will not be in vain.

Regardless of the circumstance, God's Kingdom is always advancing. There is no end to His grace, His joy, and His peace, even in our darkest canyon.

THE CHALLENGE OF VULNERABILITY

A wagon did not provide much shelter. Canvas could not protect pioneers from a well-aimed arrow or the howling winds of a winter blizzard. They were basically exposed to everything for the entire trip west. One of their great challenges was the constant vulnerability to the elements.

If the scout traveled ahead of the wagon train to secure the next section of the trail, the pioneers had to evaluate the rough data the scout had left behind. They had none of this information at the start of the trek. Only as they progressed could they gather the vital new data created by the unforeseen challenges of weather, hostilities, or equipment failure.

Every blueprint shows a completed idea or project. The blueprint is not a map showing a straight and predictable line toward completion. Obstacles and contingencies will arise as the project progresses. We can't know all of the intricate details of a trail, the needs of the travelers, or the unplanned obstructions at the start of any journey.

A lot of the stuff of life crosses our path as we implement a blueprint. Maybe we created a first draft of a map thinking it would lead us to the fulfillment of the blueprint. First drafts are just that: the first of many course corrections we will make. A slavish obedience to a first draft is never wise because it ignores the changing realities we will encounter. We will have to come to grips with the vulnerability created by constant change along the way. It is not a sign of weakness. It is simply part of any pioneering journey.

REVISITING HISTORY

On our summer trip following the historic route of the Applegate Trail, Jan and I visited the Stone Bridge along the Lost River in Southern Oregon.

When the pioneers arrived at the Lost River, they had to get their wagons across. Any river crossing required planning and wisdom. The water had to be shallow enough to not float the wagons—or else they would tip over. To find a viable crossing, pioneers often had to take a detour or backtrack.

The mountain men and First Nations people in the area told the scouts of a shallow spot to cross the Lost River, south of Klamath Falls, Oregon. To a casual observer, the river looked too deep to get wagons safely across.

But in one section, invisible to the eye, a wagon could safely roll across a natural stone bridge that spanned the river just inches below the water's surface. Today, a small irrigation dam spans the Lost River, but underneath, the Stone Bridge is still there.

Not every point of passage will be visible to the naked eye of traditional wisdom or experience. Some passageways will be discovered by researching the history of previous generations who faced the same challenge.

If we will take time to inquire of the Lord, we can find the hidden bridge or crossing. If we don't, we will suffer delay or misfortune.

God made a way for the Israelites to cross the Red Sea—a seemingly impossible crossing. When Moses stepped out in obedience to God's instructions, the waters parted, and the people safely crossed. With great celebration, they left behind stone memorials of their miraculous deliverance.

Down through history, the Israelites and other nations saw that God was always present, leading each generation through impossible barriers. But like the Stone Bridge spanning the Lost River, we won't always see these passageways at first glance.

Ask God where these crossing points are present, and He will reposition you to see what He sees.

PLANNED REST

When I read of the Applegate Wagon Train's five-month journey, I noticed that—although pressed for time—they stopped and rested along the way. These places of rest were strategically planned.

Oxen needed time to rest and graze on fresh grass. Equipment needed repair and maintenance. People needed an opportunity to simply catch their breath. These were real needs that could not be ignored.

Without these planned stops, many of the pioneers would have perished along the way. Their oxen would have died, their equipment would have stopped working, and the emotional and mental health of the group would have unraveled. Rest must be planned, or the plan will not succeed.

I recently was honored to meet a man from Australia whose name is Dave Hodgson. Dave founded the Paladin Corporation and leads *Kingdom Investors*, a worldwide teaching and training resource.

During a downturn in the economy early in his career, Dave had found himself in $76,000 of credit card debt, struggling to make ends meet. This financial descent continued until one day he and the Lord had a conversation. After God asked if Dave was willing to do business His way, Dave yielded everything. He transitioned from being just an entrepreneur to an entrepreneur with the goal of advancing God's Kingdom—not his financial portfolio. In the decades after that critical decision, Dave now owns many companies and has a financial portfolio north of one billion dollars. While his testimony is impactful, it was something he does in private that resonated with me the most.

Dave speaks at financial conferences and forums around the world. His speaking itinerary is booked out at least a year in advance. In a recent email, Dave shared that he spoke 111 times last year at various locations around the globe. He lives a very busy life, but he does something that each of us must do if we are going to survive the journey and flourish in our destination; he rests.

When Dave returns home to Australia after fulfilling a speaking itinerary, he gets on his jet ski and travels to an island off the east coast of Australia. There is no cell service or Internet available on the island. In the morning, he spears fish and barbeques them for his meals. He sits at a small camping table and transcribes the words God gives him about his personal life, his investments, and what projects to initiate.

When asked why he is so successful, Dave says the days spent on the island taking dictation and direction from the Lord have been the seedbed of his success. Without that scheduled place of rest and its resulting revelation, Dave might only be a successful entrepreneur, not a successful Kingdom entrepreneur.

MARGIN TIME

Twenty years ago, I realized that if I were to finish well, I would need to invest in things that helped me go deeper in my intimacy with God. I could then apply that intimacy to my family, friends, and workplace. The demands of my work had been taking over my calendar and daily schedule. I wanted to make an adjustment, but I did not know how or what I should do.

While I was first processing this, our church was having a weekly Wednesday night service. I would normally go into the office at 9 AM each Wednesday and stay through the evening. It made for a long day.

I remember distinctly the Lord saying, "Give me Wednesday morning." He wanted me to devote a section of time solely to Him. I began to ask Him what that would look like.

Our home in Southern Oregon is nestled in a small,

historic community surrounded by miles of hiking trails. I decided to spend my time with God on those trails each Wednesday morning. When I made the decision, my first Wednesday was still a week away, so I had time to think about what those mornings might look like.

This set-aside time would become a spiritual cartilage between me and the demands on my time. At first, I thought I should bring my Bible along on the hikes. The Lord said, *no*. Then I thought I should go up on the mountaintop and have formal devotions with Him. He said *no* again. With each suggestion, I brought to Him—to show I would be faithfully involved in some task—He said *no*. He wanted nothing from me but my presence. This was not to be a *productive* place—no tasks allowed.

As I processed this with the Lord, I finally understood that He wanted me to create a space somewhere in my week without duty—for myself or others. This was also not like my normal days off every week, usually spent with family. He wanted me to create a place where I did not study, prepare sermons, or complete any pastoral task. This time would resemble a walk with God in the cool of Eden's evening.

When that first Wednesday morning rolled around, I put on my hiking shoes and set out for the trails. I distinctly remember crossing the threshold between our town and the forest. When I entered the forest I said, "I am all yours, God." I have been saying those same words every week for the last twenty years.

This weekly hike with God has been one of the most significant times for Him to develop intimacy with me. I no longer pastor a church, and yet I still take those hikes each week. Some of the content for this book came from my margin time with God on Wednesday mornings. I hike year-round, in rain, snow, and sun. My passion to walk with Him overcomes any obstacle that might come my way. I am hungry for those few hours each week when Presence, not productivity, is the goal. In that margin time, God has affected all areas of my life, slowly realigning me with Him.

One personal impact from setting aside this time is the creativity it releases. An uncluttered mind is free to dream and pray for those things Paul described in Ephesians 3:20 that are *beyond*—things beyond all that we would ever dare to ask or think or imagine. In the beyond place of my margin time, dreams and visions are conceived.

For me, this margin time happens on my walks in the forest. For Dave Hodgson, it happens on an island. For others it might be getting on a motorcycle, or riding a bike, or sitting in a favorite chair just looking out a window after the kids are off to school. For a city dweller, it might be walking to a city park and sitting down on a bench and waiting and listening. The way you spend this time is between you and God. How and where you do it is not as important as making the time to do it.

Recently, I told a group of pastors that some of the best books being written by leaders come after they experience burnout or failure. Books written before the burnout were all about cramming more and more *good* things into someone's schedule to get the most return for the life-investment. Books written after a personal crisis invite us to pursue places that resemble a spiritual mountain trail or an island without Internet connection. In these places, the stress of life does not have a voice; these places are dedicated only to the voice of God.

Like a human knee without cartilage, we can be so bone-on-bone that we end up becoming spiritually and emotionally crippled. It is the cartilage—that cushioned space between the bones—that enables us to move with flexibility and freedom without pain. For long-term Kingdom effectiveness, each of us needs to create a margin time as a cushion between the urgencies of life and the call of God.

God is present and waiting for you in that special place if you will simply schedule the time. Your first step is to realize the importance of making space for these uncluttered encounters with Him. Put that appointment with God on your calendar as a sacred space, not to be violated by the things that create a need for this kind of space in the first place.

EXTERMINATING FATIGUE

To constantly be on the move without scheduled rest is to come to a premature end. No matter how pressing our schedule might be, rest is critical if we are going to endure the demands facing us. Rest feels dangerous to our restless souls. The act of stopping to rest will reveal the very things we are afraid to see in ourselves or in others.

Seeing something negative in our life—maybe like our need for some margin time—feels like failure and condemnation. We can spend a lifetime misinterpreting the purpose of sight and choosing not to see what is really taking place. When this happens, we allow our vision to become blinded to our reality. Sight is the beginning of healing. Sight is a sign that we are living in the light of God's brilliant presence. He is simply identifying a barrier to His goodness. That is not negative. It is needed revelation.

In a place of rest, I will recognize what can impede the long-term endurance needed to finish well. A primary root of the Hebrew word for sabbath means "to exterminate." When we stop to rest, things begin to surface in our life that have been hidden beneath a great deal of shallow surface activity. The flotsam of wrong motives and unhealthy ways of thinking begin to rise to the surface, and we see their stark and deadly reality. We must exterminate these things before they push us so hard that we collapse emotionally and spiritually from self-induced exhaustion.

If you lead a team of pioneers, it is up to you to train them to regularly schedule their rest. When the clock and calendar are stretching the emotional resources of the team, be even more proactive. When a project is at a critical stage of development, and everyone is tired and stretched to their limits, a day off together to simply have fun and enjoy each other—outside the demands of the project—might release the very thing the project needed to move past a critical juncture or deadline.

We live in a culture that drives us to experience continual forward motion. Constant motion gets falsely advertised as proof of our worth. Constant motion gets misinterpreted as significance.

Life doesn't have to be an ongoing emergency. Could this be one reason we experience so many false starts and so much frustration? Our culture has become increasingly frenetic and driven. And if our personality profile defines us as achievers, we're even more likely to propel ourselves deeper into dysfunction. We can push ourselves and our team at unhealthy speeds that are not emotionally sustainable over time. Yes, some critical junctures will occasionally appear and demand that we make an immediate response, but those times are fewer than what we have been led to believe.

Our most critical next steps are discovered through a process of disclosure and discovery only found when we choose to stop and rest. Dave Hodgson discovers this each week on an island. I experience it hiking the trails above my home. Where is your place of rest?

GO HOME

I remember stopping by our church one night to pick up something from my office. One of the pastors on our team was hard at work in his office. I stuck my head through the doorway to say hello. He looked up with tired eyes and returned my greeting with a faint smile.

I felt compelled to ask him, "Why are you here tonight?" I knew it wasn't a night scheduled for a meeting. He went on to provide a list of work-related reasons why he was not at home with his family. I told him to go home.

During our next staff meeting, I looked around the room at our team and said, "You are more important to me as people than the role you fulfill at work. I can understand needing to be here a time or two in the evening each week, but anything beyond that is too much. If I find any of you here more than that, I will tell you to pack up and go home. I need you and your family healthy more than I need you to complete your to-do list."

Even the most noble of callings can gradually take the place of what matters most. When we're lying on our deathbed, we won't be surrounded by our great achievements but by those we loved and who loved us in return. We need to guard those relationships above all else.

WORKING FROM A PLACE OF REST

For many years, Jan and I have tried to live out this principle: we work *from* rest, we don't work *to* rest. For the fifteen years I led Living Waters Church, I had the team take two consecutive days off—Friday and Saturday—so they could have extended quality family time and get some needed rest. I never wanted to give Monday to my family as a day off. I would just be tired and emotionally spent from speaking at multiple services on Sunday morning.

Jan and I used to joke that in the first five years we pioneered a church in the Rockies of Montana, I wanted to quit every Monday morning. We were in a new territory and fighting a spiritual battle that was foreign to us. It was physically and emotionally draining, and discouragement was right at our doorstep.

I discovered during those years that Monday, the traditional pastor's day off, was better spent setting my heart straight and dealing with any negative attitudes produced by a long Sunday. It turned out to be a good day to regroup and reset for the new week ahead.

SURVIVING THE JOURNEY

We can misunderstand the short-term assignment of a pioneer. Pioneers are survivalists, and they must survive a long and dangerous journey, full of immediate concerns.

But seasons of survival are not meant to be a permanent lifestyle. A survivalist mindset is exhausting if we live in it for too long. To be constantly surrounded by ongoing, monumental threats doesn't allow for an environment of rest. And without rest and the anticipation of rest, we cannot survive or prosper.

The ultimate goal of a pioneer is to transition roles to become a settler who creates a settlement. This role transition begins with the process of building a viable and prosperous community. We do this because we want to leave behind a generational inheritance.

The first winter in a new place must give way to the spring of settlement, or the vision we carried with us will never be implemented or will become lost altogether.

This applied to the first pioneers in the American West, and it applies today in any endeavor—whether it is the innovation of a new product, a church plant, or the implementation of a new educational resource. If we continually live in survival mindset, all the energy we expended on the journey will have been in vain.

THE PLAN FOR YOUR FUTURE

Jan and I just finished a twenty-year assignment. God revealed that assignment to me one morning in Athens, Greece, in 1998. He awakened me early and invited me into the kitchen of a condo where we were staying. I sat down with a cup of espresso and literally took dictation from God. That plan was then birthed in 1999 precisely nine months after its conception. Over the last 20 years, the plan God revealed to me that morning in Athens has worked out with uncanny accuracy.

We are now on the threshold of our next 20 years. This time it feels different. A measured and marked vision for the last 20 years made sense, considering how God positioned our lives during that time. The coming decades do not have the same feel.

There is a profound simplicity with this new assignment. That simplicity will enable us, and I believe some of you reading these words, to remain mobile and immediate to the voice of God's Spirit for purposes you might not have considered.

This is a Habakkuk moment of unimagined newness where our vision must be simple and immediately executable. The carrier of a new vision is to run without any burdening issues—including a cumbersome vision that hinders its own execution.

The Early Church lived day by day. They only had the moment. They also had a commission—a Great Commission—that required freedom of movement to reach the uttermost parts of Earth with the Good News. That mobile and unstructured commission would not sit well with many life-planning seminars we attend today, where we are invited to create our own future. Plans can be good, but the wrong plan can be bad.

The Early Church were not sure they would live to

see another day. Their life plan was to be immediately available to God. The dots connecting those immediate points of obedience would become the testimony of their lives that we read about in the Book of Acts.

If you are in the process of considering a pioneering journey and are feeling unsettled and a bit anxious as you consider your future, those emotions could actually be your initial response to something the Spirit is doing in you. Once you realize God is at work, the unsettled feeling and anxiety will be replaced with trust and expectancy.

In in a rapidly changing and shifting world, those two components—trusting God and expecting Him to lead you—will form your mission statement.

ASKING THE FOUR QUESTIONS

What would happen to the emotional wellbeing of any team effort if we stopped to reevaluate what was being accomplished? Every journey needs periodic recalibration.

Over the years, I have been able to lead or be part of several leadership teams. In order to be more sensitive to God's voice and His timetable, I have used a set of four questions to evaluate our progress and keep us on track. I have been using the questions for the last 25 years. They helped me and each member of our team stay focused on the essentials, as well as specific directives from God. The four questions are:

What do we like about what we are doing?

What do we not like?

What do we want to keep?

What do we want to get rid of?

Asking these four questions can be especially hard on anyone who leads through control and fears any input that might challenge their opinion. Others might ask, "If something has worked well in the past, why would we stop doing it?" What was good two years in a row might not be the fresh stirring of the Spirit for a third year. Honest evaluation spares no one of needed input, even the innovators of the original vision.

For this process of evaluation, I have learned to ask the four questions at quarterly intervals. It is wise to capture trends, and not just build a plan based on the erratic nature of the ups and downs of daily life. Weekly or monthly inquiries will not reveal these trends.

What I asked of my primary leadership team, I also have them ask of their teams. Once we recognize a trend, we can analyze it for its impact on the mission and make any adjustments. This also saves us from making assumptions.

I have seen successful enterprises ride on their current productivity, never realizing they are actually on a downward curve. I have seen successful churches fail to realize that God's favor had lifted off their model of ministry. All the surface trappings and programs were in place, but there was no sense of the Spirit's movement.

This is what futurist David Houle reminded us of when he spoke about The Shift Age. We are living in a time where we need to get light and mobile. Regular evaluation helps us offload those ways of thinking and methodologies that will inhibit our progress. It is similar to pioneers lessening the load of their wagons to navigate a challenging section of the trail.

AN ACCELERATED DISMANTLING

Perhaps one reason for much of the angst and concern in certain quarters of culture has to do with a dismantling that is taking place. God is dismantling ways of thinking, theologies, and worldviews we have accumulated in the last few generations that do not reflect His heart or His mission on Earth.

When Gutenberg invented the printing press, access to Scripture was no longer restricted to a few clerics who told people what to believe. When the Word of God was released to the masses in written form, it brought about the Reformation. In scope, impact, and immediacy, the Internet far exceeds the potential of Gutenberg's printing press. We are living in a moment of history when an accelerated dismantling of our assumptions is taking place. New insight, immediately retrievable data, and historical context are now available to us at the click of a keyboard or the tap of a touch screen.

When our familiar ideas are reexamined, we can get uncomfortable. Discomfort can quickly become fear or anger that wants to control our response to change. The things being dismantled are not sacred in God's eyes. We have made them sacred though our tradition.

Get ready for a dismantling and reconstruction of our misconceptions. We will see God do remarkable things in us and through us once we have been put back together again.

MICRO SABBATHS

One afternoon, I was running errands, and I pulled into the parking lot of a local supermarket to do some grocery shopping. When I entered the parking lot, Louis Armstrong's song "What A Wonderful World" came on the radio. I had a to-do list tugging on my time, yet I felt compelled to stay in my car and listen to the song. As I sat there listening, a deepening sense of peace came over me with each musical note and with every word. In that pause, the magnitude of my to-list faded. After the song ended, I let out a long sigh, got out of my car, and entered the store.

While pushing my shopping cart through the aisles, I processed the song and the pause with the Lord. He began to remind me of the sabbath lifestyle.

Jan and I have come to know the sabbath as a 24/7 way to think and live. It is about oneness with the One who is our Sabbath Rest. We are created to live from a place of emotional and spiritual rest. Experiencing this kind of rest is not easy, nor is it something we simply put on the calendar.

Walking through the supermarket, I was struck by how important it is for us to experience sabbath moments of rest throughout the day. I call these "micro-sabbaths." Moments when we sense the Spirit asking us to stay in our car and linger with Him just a little longer, listening to a beautiful song. Moments when we stop on the sidewalk and look up from the cement to a beautiful sunset being painted across the canvas of an evening sky. Moments of lingering in an embrace with someone you love, without hurrying the release.

Today, as you go about your life, become aware of what God is revealing in each moment of the day. We miss these moments when we think spirituality is always about moving and doing, not resting and being.

An encounter with rest may be pausing to appreciate a sound, an image, or a feeling you might normally brush past on your way forward. Follow the impressions of rest. They will lead you to a paused place where you will find a refreshing peace in your soul. Take advantage of each micro-sabbath and that moment will become a place of visitation.

SAUNTERING IN THE WILDERNESS

John Muir, the conservationist called the father of our national park system, had an interesting take on how to travel through the beauty of a forested landscape.

Muir wrote:

> *I don't like either the word [hike] or the thing. People
> ought to saunter in the mountains—not "hike!" Do
> you know the origin of that word saunter? It's a
> beautiful word. Away back in the middle ages people
> used to go on pilgrimages to the Holy Land, and
> when people in the villages through which they
> passed asked where they were going, they would
> reply, "A la sainte terre," "To the Holy Land." And
> so, they became known as sainte-terre-ers or
> saunterers. Now these mountains are our Holy
> Land, and we ought to saunter through them
> reverently, not "hike" through them.*[*]

We need to set our pace so that we can arrive at
life's destinations alive and intact as a whole and
healthy person. Life is not just about crossing the finish
line. Are you taking some time to saunter and celebrate
along the way?

DANCING THE FANDANGO

One record of the Applegate Trail documents the
moment when weary pioneers had finally navigated
the harsh desert of northern Nevada. They came to the
summit of the first lush ridge of a timbered forest
covering the Warner Mountains northwest of present-
day Cedarville, California.

When the pioneers reached the summit and saw the
expanse of green forests and the valley before them,
they danced the Fandango in celebration. Today, that
mountain pass is called Fandango Pass. Our
willingness to stop and celebrate our progress along
the way can rename a place or experience for future

---

[*] Albert W. Palmer. *The Mountain Trail and its Message.* The
Pilgrim Press. 1911.

generations.

We need to give ourselves permission to stop and dance our own version of the Fandango, celebrating our progress. Without rest, joy, and celebration, we can be overcome by the hardship of the journey and lose heart. Celebration is a holy act. Scripture tells of more feasts than fasts. Celebration is part of being a spiritually healthy person.

DRAWING THE LINE

G. K. Chesterton, the twentieth-century British theologian and philosopher, once said, "Art, like morality, consists of drawing the line somewhere."

We need to draw boundary lines to protect ourselves from the distractions and unrealistic demands of life that would keep us from what matters most. These lines define our sacred space—a place where divine foresight is unveiled at critical points.

Drawing these lines will protect us from stressors that rob us of rest and joy. Especially when we are pressed for time, a joyful celebration is often just what we need to remind us of all that God has done and is doing.

THE ENOUGH LINE

Jan and I are at the stage in life where we don't need anything more. Twenty years ago, as two missionaries returning from Europe, we stepped off the airplane with most of our earthly possessions in our luggage. We had stored a few boxes of books and Christmas decorations and a single chair in my mom's attic in Montana, but that was it.

This return home mirrored the first time we had sold everything we owned to go overseas—also returning to the US with just our luggage.

Today, in a remarkable witness of God's provision

and faithfulness, we can honestly say we need nothing. God has provided everything. We have enough.

Proverbs 23:4 tells us: "Don't wear yourself out trying to get rich. Be wise enough to know when to quit" (NLT). As soon as I finished reading those words, the Lord said, "It is important to know the meaning of enough."

We need to know what enough means for ourselves personally and corporately—for the place God assigned us in the Kingdom. I know people on both ends of the financial scale—from those with little to those with millions. God has helped many of them define what enough means for them. They have dedicated everything above the "enough line" to a purpose—to expand God's Kingdom.

Until we draw an enough line, we will waste our precious time and energy chasing after a never-enough standard of living determined for us by a consumer culture. If we never draw the line, we will look back someday and see that we wore ourselves out pursuing worthless things at the expense of worthy things.

WATCH YOUR BACK-TRAIL

On my weekly hike in the woodlands above our home, I occasionally turn around and check my back-trail. I do this for a reason.

The cougar population in Oregon has increased at an alarming rate since legislation limited the ability to manage the cougar population. One report said that before the legislation, the cougar population was approximately 1,500 in the Cascade Mountains. Now it exceeds 5,000.

Because cougars hunt in personal terrain, this has pushed young, inexperienced cougars and the old, sick ones into more populated areas in search of food. As a result, they are increasingly interacting with humans, pets, and livestock. Each time I see a hand-drawn poster for a missing pet in our neighborhood, I wonder. Just last week, a local friend posted a photo on Facebook of a group of four cougars walking down a gravel road near his home.

It always amazes me how situationally unaware some people are when walking in a forest, wearing earbuds, listening to music, oblivious to their surroundings. The same is true on city streets where even more dangerous predators walk upright on two legs.

There is a spiritual application for being aware. Not every dangerous spiritual encounter is ahead of us. Some will approach us from the back-trail of our past, waiting for an opportune moment to attack. These attacks can be in the form of a lie that says we are unworthy of forgiveness, since we just committed the same sin again after asking forgiveness for the umpteenth time. Other lies slink up behind us to tell us our failed past will become the pavement of the roadway leading to our future. Lies are opportunists that take advantage of the weakness of our unbelief.

Some of us need to do what forest service personnel advise hikers to do when they encounter a cougar. Raise your arms, shout loudly, and slowly back away. The goal is to make yourself look big and too large of a threat for the cougar to engage. The worst thing to do is run.

In the realm of the Spirit, we call this faith. It is faith in the One who stands beside us as our Redeemer. He makes us strong and courageous and spiritually large. The payment He made for us includes defanging the lies currently trailing us from behind, trying to find an opportune moment to pounce on us and sink the fangs of hopelessness deep into our soul.

Today, turn around from time to time and check your spiritual back-trail. If you see a lie, shout at it in faith. Get big in Jesus. In that moment of confrontation, you will see the lie scurry off into the forest.

FIVE QUESTIONS FOR A PIONEER

1) Can you allow yourself to be vulnerable?

Vulnerability is not normally our favorite response to life. Some see vulnerability as a negative—a weakness—and they miss its positive component. There can be a great strength in vulnerability.

Vulnerability requires us to be honest about our beliefs and feelings. It takes courage to be sensitive and acknowledge our weakness. A vulnerable and humble heart will be unguarded, tender, and open before God and others.

Life is challenging and exhausting. It can wear through the thickest skin of human strength and resistance. Something powerful takes place in the area of trust when we are honest and open. People trust truth spoken from a vulnerable heart. The strength of a team of pioneers will be seen in their ability to be vulnerable with each other. Without this vulnerability, the trail experience can become unnecessarily dangerous.

2) Are you flexible?

The path ahead will not be a straight line. It will require flexibility that can make us nervous and worried that we are deviating from the original mission. Rather than stubbornly moving into a box canyon where we will meet a dead end, a lateral move can allow us to change direction and follow a safer path. We must remain open to new ideas and be flexible enough to change direction when needed.

3) Do you believe God will make a way when no way seems possible?

Every journey will encounter the end of a visible trail. Navigating through these challenging points of passage will confirm for us that our training and personal resources are never enough to always reveal the way forward. In these critical moments, any remaining hope of human intervention evaporates. It is here that the Way-Maker will live up to His name when no way seems possible. You will never be without direction if you ask God to reveal your next step.

4) Are you intentional in learning how to rest?

Rest is a learned skill. It requires training and discipline, especially when deadlines and the expectations of others join with our fear of failure and tell us that rest will create unnecessary delays. Fight the urge to press on when rest is required. Give God a place of rest, and in that place, He will do remarkable things.

5) Is your back trail clear?

It is hard to move forward if you are living in fear of the past. We all have a past—filled with the good, bad and ugly. How you relate to the past will be determined by how confident you are in the forgiveness of God. Yes, some things prowling your back trail need to be confronted. Others simply need to be ignored.

CHAPTER 7: SETTLERS—THE CULTURE-BUILDERS

Settler: A person who settles in a new country or a colony.[*]

My friends Bobby and Beckie Haaby pastor Eagle Mountain church in Bend, Oregon. Their ministry is moving outside the walls of a church building to bring a reforming presence to the institutions of culture in their region.

This move began when Bobby approached a local businessman and asked him how he saw the Church in the Bend area. The man said one word: "irrelevant." That single, honest answer shocked Bobby, causing something to happen in his heart. It began to steer him toward the discovery of Kingdom solutions for the reformation and transformation of his city and region.

Bobby felt impressed to go to the people with influence in his city and ask them a single question, "How can we serve you?"

Some in the Church might worry that such questions can lead to aligning with ungodly lifestyles or corrupt agendas. Bobby didn't have that worry because he was acting on a word from God, and he went on to find a way to advance God's Kingdom. It was a brave, innovative, and Spirit-led approach.

The impact on the city of Bend through serving—not through force or manipulation—is a template to study

---

[*] "settler." *Collins Dictionary.* 2020. Web. 15 February 2020.

and replicate. This is how a settlement is established that will transform the surrounding wilderness of culture. When God's blueprint is offered with love and honor, great things can be accomplished.

THE GIFT OF GENERATIONAL WEALTH

After the pioneers of the Applegate Wagon Train survived their first, cold winter, they began to build a settlement; they became settlers.

Their new role required creating a sustainable community and establishing businesses, community standards, and social structures. All of this would lead to the long-term health of the settlement and a sustainable culture that could last into future generations.

There is a concept called generational wealth. This is wealth amassed by one generation and passed on to the next. While this wealth can include things like money and possessions, it is much more. If we only think of inheritance in terms of financial security, our understanding will not include the deeper inheritance of the wellbeing and prosperity of the soul of a person or culture. That kind of inheritance will leave behind a God-honoring legacy.

God desires that families prosper in body, soul, and spirit. He longs to pour out His favor and blessing on a family line. But some people's inheritance has been cut off. Due to war, premature death, mismanagement, disease, discrimination, or unresolved personal issues, a family line can be devastated within one generation, creating a challenging road of recovery for those who follow.

God desires that each of us experience a blessed life. He can return what was lost or stolen. He is able to bring back to life something that died or to create something new—something we never had to begin with. One of His greatest gifts is to take something small, like a few loaves and fish, and turn them into a feast for a multitude.

Both of our children have the gift of imagination. This is part of a generational inheritance we gave to our family. Our daughter, Anna, is an artist and published poet. In her recent nonfiction book, *Living Large on Little*, she shares principles of how to live in the largeness of God's goodness, even when our resources are limited. In the introduction, she writes:

> *This book is about spending less time seeing limitations as obstacles and...about investing in our imagination to re-see obstacles as invitations. In fact, you might say this book is about revision — re-vision.*[10]

The dividends from giving someone the freedom to imagine will release generational creativity. We can be wealthy in the eyes of the world but paupers when it comes to imagination. When Jan and I intercede for our sons and daughters—both our natural and spiritual children—we want to bless them with the freedom to imagine beyond the limitations they experience. That gift will be with them throughout their lives and beyond— leaving behind an inheritance for following generations.

Our personal prayer for the next generation is an increase above and beyond the astounding blessings God has given us. Someday, Jan and I will pass on what we have to our children. Part of that inheritance will be tangible resources, but their greatest inheritance will not be the real estate or bank account we give to them. The greatest inheritance will be in their hearts.

MULTI-GENERATIONAL FAMILY BLESSINGS

Both my parents and Jan's parents gave us an inheritance, although they weren't financially wealthy. Neither family had big bucks, mansions, or a Lamborghini in the driveway.

---

[10] Anna Elkins. *Living Large on Little*. Wordbody. 2019. 3.

Both sets of our parents survived the Great Depression. They were resilient, hardy, and without a sense of entitlement. They also handed us a spiritual heritage of love, nurturing, provision, and protection—which affected every aspect of our lives.

My dad was a carpenter. When he died, my mom stopped receiving his pension, leaving her with very little to live on apart from her meager Social Security check. Jan's folks, through no fault of their own, lost their retirement late in life. Their mission board pension program lost a majority of its portfolio through an investment error no one foresaw. Yet God intervened for both families. He restored great blessings through means not considered by most financial planners.

In their loss, our parents encountered the grace and mercy of God. Under His redemptive hand, they finished better off *after* their loss than they would have if the original plan had worked out. Their God-stories of rescue and provision are part of our inheritance. Ultimately, we have come to recognize that our inheritance comes from a higher realm than what our parents or we ourselves can pass on to the next generations.

A LESSON WE LEARNED

If one generation lacks discipline, they will negatively affect the next generation. This applies not just to lack of financial discipline but also to lack of vision discipline. Our vision of the future must be so God-centered that it can overcome our desire to sin, mismanage our money, or make foolish decisions that rob a future harvest of its greatest potential. This is how a healthy settlement is built in a family, a business, or a city.

Jan and I have made plenty of mistakes. We bought things—including new cars—"on time," by-passing financial wisdom in our decision-making process. I once read that most first-generation millionaires drive older, used cars. Instead of forking out large monthly car payments and high insurance premiums, they save money and drive an older vehicle without a budget-sapping monthly payment. These investors saved because they understood the downside of depreciation and paying interest. That wisdom took precedence over an emotional or ego-based purchase, and such decisions led them to financial freedom.

When credit cards first came out, my generation had no experience with the downside of easy debt. Before Jan and I settled down to start a family, we charged our first credit card to the max, "buying" a cruise to the Caribbean. It took only that one poor decision for reality to hit home. It also took several years to pay off the mistake.

If we approach wealth as a way to gain more things and status, we model a lack of financial character and jeopardize prosperity for coming generations. This will squander our ability to create and pass on healthy generational wealth.

When I consider a purchase or a choice, I take a moment to inquire of the Lord. I also envision my wife and children. It's amazing how that image—that imagination—will affect my decisions. As my family comes to mind, so do those who have trusted me and my voice as a spiritual father. Ultimately, that quest for discernment will lead me to the wisdom of God.

When I was young man still struggling with my role as a husband and father, I didn't always make good decisions. And though I am still not perfect in this process, I want to leave behind something tangible for my children.

I also want to leave behind the blessings of my relationship with God and the years of my personal discipleship. Most importantly, I want to leave behind a testimony of God's grace and mercy that will create the foundation of a healthy settlement for future generations.

SETTLEMENTS CREATE POINTS OF MEASUREMENT

On June 4, 1851, three men laid a stone in the west hills of Portland, Oregon that would later become known as the Willamette Stone.

The Willamette Stone was used as the initial point of reference for all future land survey measurements taken in Oregon, Washington, and parts of western Idaho. Present day surveyors still use the reference point created by the Willamette Stone to locate old boundary markers and to settle land disputes.

The Willamette Stone was the by-product of creating a settlement. The culture we create today will become the reference point for future generations. Generations far ahead in the future will refer back to the measurements of honor and trust that we lay down.

Every healthy settlement will have its own version of the Willamette Stone. Each stone establishes the values forged by the settlement's first generation.

THE ARCHAEOLOGY OF CULTURE

It's been 50 years since Woodstock took place at Yasgur's farm on a grassy hillside outside Bethel, New York. 400,000 young people showed up to listen to Janis Joplin, Jimi Hendrix, The Grateful Dead, and many others sing the songs of an emerging generation. It was an iconic moment in American history.

I recently read that a team of archaeologists excavated the meadow where the concert occurred, looking for the original sites of the vendor booths, main stage, and sound towers.

Every culture will leave behind a debris trail. The things we cast away can tell the story of what took place and the context in which it happened. In the field of archaeology, context tells as much of the story as an artifact being discovered.

If a team of spiritual archaeologists were to arrive and

dig around in the remnants of our lives, what would they find? In their research, they would discover the context of our life—the good and the bad of our settlement. That discovery would reveal the history of a life well-lived or one that missed the God-given opportunities to create a healthy culture able to survive the lifespan of the first generation of a settlement.

Settlers who lived in history and settlers living today need to evaluate the evidence they are creating by their lives. What they leave behind will tell a story.

THE POWER OF BELONGING

I've heard experts suggest that the depression and loss of hope we see in our western culture stems primarily from a lack of belonging. When given a chance to experience belonging within a group, depression decreases—and in some cases disappears. A weary and unsettled person—someone always on the move, without the peace that comes from building something of lasting value and enjoying its fruit—is headed for despair.

Perhaps the emotional gift of community and a sense of belonging exceeds the success of the settlement itself. We all need to feel like we belong to a family, a team, or a community.

I can only imagine what it felt like when weary pioneers finally became part of a community who lived in warm cabins with crackling fires in the stove and the smell of dinner cooking. The memories of weariness of the trail would turn into gratitude for what they had established.

Such a settler might look out in the distance and see the rising smoke from a neighbor's chimney—someone also enjoying the reward of their journey. This community would experience the comfort of knowing their neighbors would be there to help if they needed it. Community creates a sense of security that is only available when we know we belong to each other.

If you have a role in creating health in the settlement of a corporation, family, or local community, one of your greatest achievements will be to create a sense of belonging. Belonging becomes a powerful adhesive that holds a community together, especially when facing seasons of discontent and fear. Jesus asked twelve men to follow Him who belonged before they believed in a traditional sense, and the world was forever changed because of that gift of belonging.

FINANCIAL PROVIDER

For the last 46 years of marriage, I have wanted to provide a life for Jan that would give her security and comfort. That meant going to work when I didn't feel like it. It meant getting enough life insurance just in case I passed away before the kids were raised and our home was paid off. It also meant saving for retirement and doing all the other things required of a faithful husband and father. It gave me great comfort to know Jan would have enough financial security to live comfortably in case I was no longer present. These are the things we expect a man to do who loves his wife and family. This happens when we leave behind our boyhood and engage the responsibilities of manhood.

Every man should try to do these things to the best of his ability, but there is something more important that I discovered along the way as I tried to fulfill my commitments. I discovered it was God in His great faithfulness who carried us through the last 46 years of marriage when life did not work out as we had planned. It was His generosity that surprised us with more than enough at the most unexpected moments. It was God who sustained us through the tough years when we didn't have enough to live on, save, or invest. He was there when our best-laid plans failed miserably and left us with little to show for our efforts.

When I failed and discovered the depths of my

immaturity and ignorance, I discovered that it was me—not God—restricting or limiting His expressions of love. He was always there for me, patiently waiting for me to return to Him.

A SETTLEMENT WILL REPURPOSE OUR LIVES

Our daughter, Anna, lives in a small loft apartment. It is a classy place, with a claw-foot tub, skylights, and unique furnishings she has collected over the years. Anna decorated it as only an artist and poet could.

When Anna was creating the loft, she found a 100-year-old barn that was being torn down. She asked if she could have some of the barn wood to use as flooring for her loft. It was my job to plane each plank. After the resurfacing was complete, we discovered beautiful wood grains and textures below the weathered surface. We installed and then stained the planks.

The texture and color of the wood flooring made the loft pop with beauty and class. Anna then gathered small, smooth river stones and placed them in the empty knotholes in the planks. The finished product is a truly original creation. It became a piece of architectural artwork.

The process of repurposing the barn wood siding reminds me of what happens when we arrive and settle down to enjoy the reward of a successful journey. The hardships of the trail weather us. After we arrive, the Lord begins to repurpose our lives. He planes away the painful things that marked us in the journey and masked the beauty of His creation. When God's work is done, we are ready for installation in a new place.

That repurposed place will cause others to stop and comment on the beauty of your life, not realizing where that beauty came from. You will become a living testimony that—with God—everything can have a new and repurposed potential.

FIVE QUESTIONS FOR A SETTLER

1) Do you value the settler assignment?

We have romanticized the role of scouts and pioneers, but we tend to think of settlers as those who settle for something less. In reality, the purpose of the scouting and pioneering phase of a journey is to get to the destination where a sustainable culture can be built. Creating a settlement is the goal of the journey.

2) Do you understand the components of a healthy settlement?

A healthy, viable community requires obvious things like clean water, healthy food, a solid infrastructure, and sound government. But you also have to consider the spiritual and emotional health of the settlement. Things like honor and the fruit of the Spirit create healthy relationships in a community.

While you work on the natural infrastructure of a city, government, or a business venture, do not forget the more important spiritual and emotional components. A settlement dies a slow and painful death when community dysfunction goes unchallenged.

3) Is your settlement creating generational inheritance?

Everything you do should be transferrable to the next generation. The ceiling of your accomplishments will become the floor the next generation walks upon. Some great ideas die in a single generation because they were not passed on. Every choice you make will have a ripple effect.

4) Does your settlement create a sense of belonging?

A sense of belonging is one of the most powerful of human emotions. It's what brought the prodigal son home to his father. It's what binds a family and community together, and it's what gives us the ability to rebound after failure. Without a sense of belonging, we will become a shallow expression of true living—even if our dream or idea succeeds.

5) Can you live in a settlement and not settle?

Being a settler is actually more challenging in the long term than being a scout or pioneer because you go deeper, not just farther. Staying in place and working through the day-to-day details of a settled life with the same view out the front window can appear less romantic or adventurous than being out in the wild, discovering new trails, or following a dream through challenging but interesting terrain. But in these settlement phases, some of the greatest progress can occur.

When forward motion ceases, those who have never learned to rest will set out again to recapture that feeling of motion. They will step away from building the potential for generational influence and will eventually find themselves in a place of sorrow because there was nothing to leave behind except wanderlust.

Every sphere of society is created to have a secure, caring community in order to flourish. When we abandon the value of community, we will end up carrying a dream without a destination.

CHAPTER 8: PREPARING FOR THE JOURNEY

The Lord typically gives me a word to carry for each season. The word I am carrying in this season is "reset." God is currently resetting the course of individuals, businesses, ministries, and governments. Without a reset, we will enter the next season guided by assumption from the past, not revelation for the future.

This reset is actually part of an equation that will help us receive strategic revelation to set our course for the next leg of our journey:

Reset + Refocus + Rest = Revelation

RESET

A reset takes us back to the original intent or meaning of something. This is not going back into history. It is actually resetting us in the present in order to create a new history under the guidance of God's Spirit.

We can too easily drift away from God's original intent and then stall. We have not been called to live in a static representation of Kingdom life. Just before each new season, God will reset our priorities to His original blueprint. He does this to get us moving once again, motivated by His original intent.

REFOCUS

After a reset, new opportunities will refocus our efforts. This refocusing will create simplicity, helping to highlight the specific things God has called each of us to do. It will require that we say *no* to some things currently on our plate and *yes* to things we had not considered before the refocusing took place.

REST

A place of rest is where God does His most significant work in us. If we are willing to learn how to rest, we will experience a depth of faith not known in a restless place. God gives us the power and authority to engage in greater exploits in His Kingdom from a place of rest. This rest is purposeful, calendared, and sacred.

This rest is more than just taking a day off each week. It must become a lifestyle, a constant way of thinking and living. Rest reveals the God-solutions that a stressed and burned out mind cannot perceive. Rest will be the place from which the next revival and reformation will be birthed.

We enter this place of rest when we choose to lay down our undisciplined ambition and our need to always have to produce to validate a lesser identity. We will enter this place of rest through a gauntlet of mocking voices and self-doubt. Those who cross the threshold and enter rest will step into the arena of belief in the God of miracles.

REVELATION

Revelation is the product and goal of the completed equation. This is not a repetition of past revelations. It builds upon what has been shown in the past. It adds new insight not previously considered before the reset, refocus, and rest occurred. These are divine breakthroughs of revelation.

Fear, especially of the unknown, will be our greatest enemy if we allow it to have a voice and remain unchallenged. Fear never has a place in any spiritual math we might calculate. We will need to intentionally exchange our fear for the certainty of God's love. He will walk with us through this equation if we ask Him for help and obey His instructions.

REDUCTION & REFITTING

Imagine you were a family living in the Midwest in the 1800s. You have a home, a livelihood, friends, and cherished possessions. At some point, you know your future is out West. The journey will require you to sell your home and most of your possessions, and—worst of all—that you say a tearful goodbye to friends and family. You then have to fit everything you will carry with you into the freight box of a wagon.

These early pioneers made difficult and painful decisions. They only took with them the barest of possessions, without a guarantee they would arrive safely to the place of their dreams. They had to leave everything nonessential behind.

Jan and I have been through the process of reduction several times in the last 46 years of marriage. We just went through another type of reduction, not of our possessions, but in our thinking about the Kingdom of God and the Church. We needed to get ready for this new era.

Without leaving behind some old ways of thinking, and without adopting new mindsets, we would not be able to navigate the canyons and dry desert stretches that are part of every journey. In God's Kingdom, reduction prepares us for the possession of greater things that hands filled with things of lesser value cannot carry.

SIMPLIFYING DEFINITIONS

After decades of pastoring, I had accumulated a lot of emotional, spiritual, and intellectual baggage. Anyone who has served a single mission over time is affected in this way, no matter what your field.

I realized I needed to simplify, and in some cases offload things I had carried for a long time. A few years ago, I received an invitation to speak at a conference on reformation. This was not the historic Reformation of 1517 with Martin Luther, but the reformation of culture currently taking place within the "Seven Mountains" concept. This concept invites the Church to become an influencing presence in the seven spheres of cultural influence: Government, Religion, Education, Economy, Arts & Entertainment, Media, and Family.

One of the first things the Lord had me do was to simplify all aspects of my message, reducing each element to a single, simple expression. I wanted to create one of those elevator pitches I mentioned earlier. I wanted to capture people's interest in an aspect of the Great Commission that they might not have considered. They could go deeper into these subjects during later times of personal reflection and study. The elevator pitch was also a metaphor for the simplification I was experiencing personally in this reset.

REDEFINING & RESHAPING

One of the first things the Lord asked me to redefine and reduce was the description of the equipping gifts of Apostle, Prophet, Evangelist, Pastor, and Teacher (Ephesians 4). There is a raft of insightful teaching available to us from gifted theologians on these gifts and their purpose in the Church. As useful as those materials are, they don't work well in the marketplace.

Once again, I found myself simplifying. God was changing my vocabulary.

I remember the day when the Lord gave me a simplified definition of the five equipping gifts. That simplification has opened up unique and engaging conversations with people.

Here is the essence of the five equipping gifts:

- *Apostles* receive Heaven's blueprint.
- *Prophets* announce the blueprint.
- *Evangelists* recruit human resources to the blueprint.
- *Pastors* create the environment where the blueprint can grow and flourish.
- *Teachers* take the blueprint and expand it into a schematic form, teaching each point and how all the parts work together.

Not long after compiling this, I read I Corinthians 12:27-28 while considering the simplification of my understanding of the equipping gifts:

> *Now you are Christ's body, and individually members of it. And God has appointed in the church, first apostles, second prophets, third teachers, then miracles, then gifts of healings, helps, administrations, various kinds of tongues* (NASB).

I always thought this was some kind of ecclesiastical stacking order with apostles occupying the top spot. But the Lord said, "Look at the word 'first.'"

I went to my language resources. I discovered that in this context, "first" is not hierarchal. It simply means first in sequence. The apostle starts everything off by receiving a heavenly blueprint detailing Kingdom expansion. The other gifts will follow—not always in order, but in the sequence as needed under the direction of the Spirit.

GOD RETRAINED MY EARS

In the process of being reset, I did not read the Bible for 18 months. I listened to it. I choose the *New Living Translation* because it is a dynamic equivalence translation. It was written to be heard in the way someone who sat in the original audience might have heard Scripture.

I wanted to experience how a first-century believer would respond to one of Paul's letters being read in a home church gathering. Many of those early audiences were not fully illiterate, so listening was the only way they could "read."

Since God does not require an advance degree in theology to understand his heart, I decided to also stop reading word studies, commentaries, and human opinion during those 18 months. I simply wanted to hear the Word delivered in its original form and presentation.

That first early morning when I sat in my living room, I felt a bit uncomfortable not having a Bible in my lap. It was just me, an audio file, and a listening ear.

As the narrator spoke, I imagined sitting in a home group meeting in Ephesus 2,000 years ago. I tried to listen as if I had just heard from friends that one of Paul's letters had arrived. I captured that excitement and expectation as I sat and simply listened.

What happened was so refreshing. The Scripture came alive in a new way—a way I had not experienced in years. A key contributor to that freshness was the simplicity of what I was hearing. It was not congested with opinions and a library full of study aids. It was raw and beautiful Scripture. The simplicity created a settling in my soul—a settling that comes when we return to original intent.

GOD RETRAINED MY EYES

Another aspect of retraining took place a few summers ago when Jan and I did not go to church for five weeks. Previous to that, we had been in church whenever the doors were open...for forty years. That is a long time.

We decided to take a "staycation." We live in a quaint little town where tourists from around the world come to visit. We had a built-in vacation spot.

We felt directed by the Lord to see what life on Sunday mornings looked like outside the walls of the Church. So, on Sunday mornings, we rode our bicycles into town to visit outdoor markets and coffee shops and cruise through the neighborhoods.

We were not forsaking the gathering together as the writer of Hebrews warned. This was not five weeks of abandonment. It was five weeks on assignment to receive fresh insight.

It was strangely refreshing to see a world I did not know existed. We got to see and hear another slice of our culture. I saw families with smiles on their faces walking through the outdoor market and past the gift shops and cafés. It seemed that people were emotionally exhaling after a busy week of noses pressed to the proverbial grindstone.

I even saw a few people from our church, smiling and waving at me as I bicycled by, offering my own wave and a smile in return. Some of the people I saw walking through our small town on Sunday mornings were not running away from God or ignoring Him. They were resting.

I knew many of these people worked long hours each week—50, 60 and even 70 hours. When Saturday rolled around, they had to spend much of the day catching up on family to-do lists. Sunday morning was the one day of rest these people had.

Sunday morning Church gatherings have great value. I honor these gatherings. In fact, during one of them many years ago, God transformed my life. I am also glad for the emergence of different days, times, and venues for gatherings, especially for those who need community but can't attend a Sunday morning service. Church is so much more than Sunday morning.

We need to validate good choices to gather outside church buildings like we validate the gatherings inside them. After all, Jesus said, "For where two or three have gathered together in My name, I am there in their midst" (Matthew 18:20 NASB). That kind of freedom can be unsettling to leaders who have linked their identity to a full sanctuary on Sunday morning.

God always wants to enlarge our current understanding of how the Church is to function and interact with culture. He is retraining our eyes to see people and their needs through the lens of mercy. Sometimes, that clarity only comes when we step out of our normal routine to see where the people we want to serve really live.

DEFINING THE CHURCH

When someone considers the word "church," they probably imagine a building with pews, pulpits, and pastors. There is nothing wrong with that description unless it represents the total expression of what it means to be the Church.

The Greek word *ekklesia* translates into English as "church." When that word was first used in the New Testament, it had already been in use for centuries, but not in a religious context. *Ekklesia* was used in both Roman and Greek cultures to define an influence taking place in the marketplace of culture. It was a secular, governmental word.

The *ekklesia* in Greek culture was the ruling body that governed a city or state. During Jesus' lifetime, the Romans controlled Israel, having replaced the Greeks as the dominate power, but they held on to the Greek concept of *ekklesia*. Israel saw *ekklesia* as a secular, governmental body that directed the course of culture.

When Paul wrote letters to the saints in a city, he was writing to all of them—the *ekklesia*. God planted His Church into the social fabric of a city, not into a structure on the city's main street that only met a few times each week. The *ekklesia* was already positioned in places of influence, wherever they lived and worked. Their presence shifted the influence of each sphere of culture toward a Kingdom mindset and way of living. When the Church did gather, they met in homes, mostly around meals. Their gatherings were celebrations of communion, worship, testimony, and teaching that encouraged and instructed.

When Paul planted a church in a city, he did so knowing that the salt and light they brought to their particular sphere of influence would initiate change. Perhaps the most poignant insight came from Julian the Apostate, the last pagan emperor of Rome. Julian wrote:

> *These impious Galileans not only feed their own, but ours also, welcoming them with agape, they attract them, as children are attracted with cakes. Whilst the pagan priests neglect the poor, the hated Galileans devote themselves to works of charity, and by a display of false compassion have established and given effect to their pernicious errors. Such practice is common among them and causes contempt for our gods.*[11]

This could only happen if the Church—the *ekklesia*—was embedded in culture, especially since persecution was rampant, and public gatherings were dangerous. Julian's dying words say it all: "You

---

[11] *Epistle to Pagan High Priests.*

Galileans have conquered!"[12] The conquering was accomplished by their love and service to all the people of their city, no matter what day of the week.

EXPLORING NEW STRUCTURES

Another area God wanted to reset in my life was how I viewed leadership structures. He wanted me to reconsider and expand the structure I used to express the Church and her mission.

When I stepped more deeply into the reset process, the Lord took me on a journey to discover the global impact of a reformer—not just in the Church but in culture.

What would it be like to belong to a group of people who worked together to help a people, a city, and a nation prosper? That is a worthy calling with a worthy destination. The more I studied the subject, the more I came to realize two things would need to be addressed for this reformation to take place.

First, our current understanding of eschatology (the study of the end of time) would be challenged. Many of us grew up with an ominous outlook at what we called the "end times." We were taught that a dark culmination of time was coming and that things would get progressively worse until then. Social statistics are revealing the reality that our world is actually getting better, not worse.

We thought God's judgment was a form of punishment instead of a loving boundary He set for our safety and good. We saw the Church flying up and away into glory leaving behind a hopelessly decaying world. I have come to see that God had something else in mind—something better.

We can anticipate goodness to overcome decay

---

[12] Theodoret. *Historia Ecclesiastica*. 3:35.

because God's justice makes wrong things right. As a reformation gains more traction, each sphere of culture will be transformed for the better.

We should no longer wait to be ejected from the challenges of this world. We have been commissioned to work in concert with God's Spirit to form Kingdom alliances that will transform nations into flourishing examples of God's love. Jesus would never have instructed His disciples to pray, "On Earth as it is in Heaven" if that were not a possibility.

There is no end to the increase of God's government and His peace. Regardless of your circumstance, His Kingdom is always advancing: there is no end to His government—there is no retreat or loss, there is no end to His mercy, there is no end to His joy and peace (Isaiah 9:7, my paraphrase).

CHANGING STRUCTURE

The structure of the Church is changing. Many people are no longer content to simply sit Sunday after Sunday in a worship gathering without being able to bring significant change to the brokenness we see in the world. People want to intentionally and personally engage with a mission of Kingdom significance. They are looking for a culture-altering move of God's Spirit that will transform the world in measurable ways.

Increasing numbers of people have moved beyond a singular expression of the Church. They have not left the Church but they *have* left the narrow expression of the Church we have offered to them.

One of the more astute visionaries of the Seven Mountain concept and the Church's role in culture is Johnny Enlow. Johnny and his wife, Elizabeth, lead a ministry called Restore7. Johnny wrote an article on his blog describing what takes place when we live in an either/or mindset in the Church:

We have two ditches to avoid. On one side of the road is the ditch of "in the millennium—one day God—after the rapture" perspective. That is a disempowering ditch that is the "old guard's" territory-ceding narrative....The ditch on the other side of the road is self-determinism and self-empowerment. It says, "God is not going to do anything and so WE had better unite and do what needs to be done because that is how God does things." This is just as dangerous of a ditch and it is delusional "self- empowerment.

Many proponents of 7 Mountains perspectives tend toward this approach as the cure to the other ditch—but it is just another ditch. Neither Caleb nor David was mighty because they sufficiently believed in themselves, or even in Israel's ability to unite and defeat the enemy. Their gifting was in SEEING GOD and His accompanying story-line—not in their Type A, self-deterministic personality, which tends toward orphan-like thinking, where you are relying totally on yourself.

When you are SEEING properly (20/20 vision), everyone is in perspective—you, the enemy, and God. YOU have participation. The enemy is the least important detail, but his comparative size TO US is designed to shock us out of "self-help" into a search for God. The God-view is the most important. He is neither absent nor totally accomplishing everything without you. He fights your battles, but responsive obedience that shows you see Him is required. Without Him you can do nothing. With Him all things are possible.[13]

[13] Johnny Enlow. "2020: A Year of Roaring Justice and Raging Hope." *Restore7*.
https://www.restore7.org/blog/2020/1/7/2020-a-year-of-roaring-justice-and-raging-hope. Web. 24 February 2020.

The reformation currently underway is bringing to the Church what Johnny Enlow mentioned in his article: a new perspective. With that perspective will come an invitation for us to participate with God in what He is doing within each culture to influence them toward positive, Kingdom-based change. How we see God in all of this will determine our response, whether we become a reforming voice or remain silent. When all is said and done, God will have His way. Our hope is in the God who is the Way-Maker. All else will fall short.

LEADERSHIP STRUCTURES & FUNCTIONS

Another area needing adjustment is our understanding of leadership functions and structures. For example, I shared earlier that we can have a vertical form of leadership structure. The people higher up the totem pole can be perceived as having more value because they are leading from the top. The Lord never meant for us to have a top-down hierarchy in our leader structures. His definition has always been a servant-leader model. He sees us in a spiritual family, raising up sons and daughters who will become fathers and mothers. God is first and foremost a Father, not a Type-A personality CEO.

My journey into leadership structures enhanced my understanding of another familiar verse:

> *Together, we are his house, built on the foundation of the apostles and the prophets. And the cornerstone is Christ Jesus himself* (Ephesians 2:20 NLT).

Apostles lay down a blueprint that initiates a process of Kingdom expansion. They invite other equipping gifts to step into the blueprint to fulfill their unique roles. This does not always happen in a clear and predictable order.

We are each called to lay down our lives for the cause of Christ. Along with that personal investment, we are also called to lay down a hierarchal form of leadership. Kingdom leadership is a horizontal structure, putting all boots on the ground at the same time, allowing people the freedom to run at the speed of their faith.

A vertical structure can only increase by addition at the bottom. A horizontal structure produces a multiplication of growth, because all participants belong and are moving together. A leader with an apostolic gift will move first in sequence and then for a season will build and establish a settlement of faith. Other leadership gifts may continue to explore beyond the apostolic gift. The "first in sequence" definition applies to the initial stages of a vision, but it is not a hard and fast rule once the blueprint is put in place. All exploration happens in stages, and it is not always done in a linear, out-in-front fashion.

Wagon masters in the American West rode up and down long strings of wagons—sometimes twenty miles long—making sure everyone was moving in unison toward the goal. These wagon-train apostles did not always stay at the head of the train. Their apostolic role was all-encompassing for the mission and added to the safety and confidence of those making the journey.

Our assignment is to lead like Jesus, who did not abuse, manipulate, or control from the top of a leadership totem pole. In fact, true leadership is defined in the context of family and marriage in Ephesians 5, beginning with verse 23:

> For the husband is the head of the wife just as Christ is the head of the Church, the body of which he is the Savior" (NRSV).

There are different meanings for the word translated as "head" in Scripture. In Ephesians 5, "head" does not mean the "lead" or the "first." In this context, a good definition is "scout." It refers to Jesus as the one who went ahead of us, ready to lay down His life for us. True leadership is sacrificial and lays down its life for others.

When we came to Medford twenty years ago to pastor Living Waters Church, the Lord gave Jan and me a clear word. Not only had He given us a twenty-year timeline, but He also asked us to hold the church with open hands. We were to make preparations at the beginning to hand off the ministry to our spiritual sons and daughters who had not yet appeared on the scene. This would involve creating a structure and environment where succession was not an obstacle but a celebrated opportunity.

God was speaking to me about being a spiritual father to my generation. That handoff began immediately through intercession. Jan and I began to pray for those leaders to be revealed to us. We also asked God to help us finish well in this assignment and for the church to transition well. We knew how impossible it would be to accomplish this task on our own—in our own strength and wisdom.

LEADING BY EXAMPLE

Setting the stage for a healthy future transition requires that we model that preferred outcome long before it arrives. I remember one day when our entire team sat around my office for a quarterly planning session. I offered what I thought was a great idea. I wanted everyone to have liberty in their response, without worrying that they might step on my preference.

As my idea made its way around the room and each person gave their input, it became increasingly obvious that while my plan had merit, its application was short-sighted. I let out a sigh of relief when the idea finally arrived back in my lap. My relief came from knowing that we had become a team of individuals who were confident enough to tell each other what we really thought and to do so with honor. We did not worry that our honest assessments would affect our relationship.

At that time, our team represented all five of the equipping gifts. While I had the lead role under a structure set by our denomination, I was not interested in being on top of the decision-making heap. I valued the team's input too much. I did not lead by consensus but by a word from the Lord. However, each member of our team saw things from a different perspective, which made for better decisions—both in substance and in timing.

Leaders need to be given a free rein to make decisions and offer opinions. A spiritual parent allows risk and the opportunity to make mistakes in an environment of trust and honor without the fear of rejection. Spiritual fathers and mothers equip their spiritual sons and daughters to do the same.

YOUR COMING REVEAL

God is creating connections, alliances, and partnerships with those who realize the current expression of the Church will need to become more agile.

During the Azusa Street Revival of the early 1900s, people came from all over the world to be touched mightily by God. The Azusa gathering was not tightly structured and bound. In that environment, the Spirit was free to move—releasing a global impact. That era also became known as a great missionary movement, as revival swept around the world. The result was the transformation of nations.

Today, the revealing of these agile individuals and

groups will be the result of a winnowing currently taking place in the Church. Those who are part of these world-changing groups will be able to move at the speed and impulse of the Spirit. They are being called out from circular orbits of effort that are unable to think outside the gravitational pull of the status quo. They will not have to ask permission from those at the top of the totem pole of a religious hierarchy.

GIFTS OF ACCESS

A familiar translation of Proverbs 18:16 reads, "A man's gift makes room for him and brings him before great men (NKJV)." This verse has been interpreted to mean that our personal ministry gifts opened a way for us to gain access to important relationships that a non-gifted person wouldn't be able to enter. While that can be true, it is not what the verse is saying.

That same word translated as "gift" in Proverb 18 is used elsewhere in Scripture to describe the dowry given for a marriage. It is the generosity of an offering given to God as an act of worship. It is a gift given to a ruler as a gesture of goodwill. It is also a gift given in secret to pacify someone's anger. In the original usage, it had nothing to do with ministry gifts.

The misunderstanding of this gift has led to an unhealthy, elitist mentality—the idea that only certain people with certain gifts can be used by God to speak to those in places of authority and importance.

In actuality, that verse is about wisdom. Offering a gift can open a relational door and provide an opportunity to deliver a spiritual gift. Any of us—not just those who possess a profound spiritual gift—can deliver these spiritual gifts from a place of wisdom.

A more current translation of Proverbs of 18:16 reads: "Would you like to meet a very important person? Take a generous gift. It will do wonders to gain entrance into his presence (TPT)." If we are being led by God to meet with someone in a place of authority, we should prepare a gift to bring with us; it could be a kind word or something tangible. The gift will open the door to grant us the favor of an audience where a spiritual gift can then be delivered.

FOCUS & ACCELERATION

A horizontal leadership structure has another benefit. It creates focus and acceleration. Jan and I were driving through some remote sections of southeast Oregon. I love the immense expanse of sagebrush and old weathered barns out there. These look like the "wide open spaces" of the old westerns I grew up watching. You can travel for miles before you see any sign of human settlement.

What I did see were roadside caution signs like, "Open Range: Watch for Livestock on the Road." I also saw remote wooden corrals with loading chutes and ramps. These corrals are used to round up cattle before the arrival of winter snow.

After passing several corrals, I began to think of prodigal children, wayward friends, and disconnected relationships needing restoration. I also thought of people who need to be rounded up in love and focused on a common mission in community. These disconnected ones roam on the open range of their free will, living with unrealized potential in isolation.

God is placing a spiritual corral on the open range of relationships. He is restoring households, estranged family members, and disconnected business partnerships. He knows how to find these disenfranchised ones in the distant outback and round them up. He will corral them for a *kairos* moment of restoration and acceleration. God's corral will narrow their options like a loading chute used to round up cattle and deliver them into a new pasture they thought impossible.

THE FOCUS OF NATIONS

Jesus said to His disciples: "All authority has been given to Me in Heaven and on Earth. Go therefore and make disciples of all nations" (Matthew 28:18-19 NASB). Jesus preached the Gospel of the Kingdom. That Kingdom message is our biblical mandate and what we need to explore.

The nation of Israel had a calling to share God's grace and favor with a world unaware of Him. The prophet Isaiah regrets their failure to do so (Isaiah 26:10-15). But he also prophesies that one day, the nations will hear the Good News and come streaming to God.

I see the life of faith much differently today than when I first became a pastor. I once saw the Church focused on what has been described as the Gospel of Salvation. The salvation of every human being is our main goal, but there is an added, essential element some of us missed. That missing element is the discipling of nations. While we continually work to introduce people to Jesus, once they are a follower of Christ, we need to help them focus on the Great Commission mandate: the discipling of nations.

Discipled nations are the result of discipled individuals. In my current understanding, I am seeing the teachings of Jesus and His Kingdom with fresh eyes because I am standing at a new vantage point that has a wider field of view. It is a global vision.

Every follower of Christ has a role to play in this Kingdom enterprise. Remember the Seven Mountains? Those spheres of influence are waiting for you. If you own a small business, you have a valued and critical role in the sphere of Economy. If you are in the entertainment industry, you can have great influence and affect positive change in the sphere of Arts & Entertainment. If you are a single mother who works two jobs while raising your children, you can have a significant impact in the Family sphere—and in your workplace.

I have a young friend, Joey LeTourneau, who is running for a congressional seat in the State of California. As I write this, the election is still months away. Joey and I have met a few times to talk about his platform and the challenges he faces running for an elected office for the first time.

Joey saw a need for another voice in the race—a voice speaking Kingdom values for what is good and right and just for all people. He desires to move away from the current divide created by warring political factions. His platform is refreshing and has, at its core, the hope to see all people flourish and prosper. I applaud Joey's commitment.

We can see the problems facing our world and fail to realize that God has asked each of us to step up in our own unique way and become part of the solution. Joey decided that he could make a difference in the sphere of Government, so he threw his hat in the ring. He is like many who have a Davidic anointing to step forward and challenge the formidable giants of culture.

I have another friend, George Palo, who lives in the African nation of Zambia. George is an astute man and an apostolic leader in his nation. He is regularly invited to speak to those in the highest positions of government. His input is valued because it offers the possibility of a positive Kingdom transformation for his nation—not the failed and self-serving policies of the past. His contributions are often given in private meetings behind closed doors. In those meetings, he is sharing the heart of God to government officials, and that revelation is steering his country in a new and hope-filled direction.

The next great move of God in the Western Church will involve every sphere of society. We will find creative ways to go beyond the Gospel of Salvation to engage the larger mission represented in the Gospel of the Kingdom.

Isaiah prophesied about this and Jesus declared it in Luke 4:18 (TPT):

> *"The Spirit of the Lord is upon me, and he has anointed me to be hope for the poor, freedom for the brokenhearted, and new eyes for the blind, and to preach to prisoners, 'You are set free!' I have come to share the message of Jubilee, for the time of God's great acceptance has begun."* Then Jesus added, *"These Scriptures came true today in front of you."*

ALL GIFTS WORKING TOGETHER

The larger a group gets, the more you will see all three roles of scout, pioneer, and settler working together at the same time. Think about Apple and the creation of the iPhone. Apple has scouts who are constantly looking for new ways to expand the original blueprint of the iPhone concept. Pioneers are taking those new concepts on a journey toward implementation. The settlers are creating a sustainable culture for their product. This progression happens in any sphere of influence where something has developed beyond the first generation of an idea and continues to expand.

I can see all three gifts working together in my good friends, James and Anna Kramer. They developed a global technology platform called Commissioned. It is designed for the purpose of connecting ministries and corporate visionaries from all spheres of cultural influence. Their goal is to become a visible representation of God's heart expressed on Earth.

The Kramers developed Commissioned out of a dream to bring together Kingdom-minded leaders and entrepreneurs to accelerate the Great Commission. I have watched their beginning vision come alive, and it is a joy to have seen all three roles of scout, pioneer, and settler at work through their lives and ministry.

FLOURISHING NATIONS

Jan and I have friends who represent innovative technologies that have the potential to change the trajectory of nations. They not only have the blueprints, patents, and ability to accomplish these things, but most importantly, they have an understanding of God's heart as the foundational purpose of their mission.

The word this group uses to define their combined effort is "flourish." These wonderful people want nations to flourish. They feel called by God to help individual nations reach their greatest potential by bringing Heaven to Earth, individually and nationally.

This ministry is a spiritual version of Maslow's famous hierarchy of needs. Meeting the most basic human needs of food, water, warmth, and shelter is part of the Gospel of the Kingdom. Jesus said to feed the poor, clothe the naked, and care for others like we would want someone to care for us in our time of need. That kind of love creates a trust equity.

People whose physical needs are met will be able to hear God's message of love more easily than when their stomachs are empty.

Leslie Keegel leads a national church movement in Sri Lanka. He said his ministry mission is to love people, until they ask him why. The "why" of the church's compassion will connect people to God's love.

One of the most powerful testimonies of national transformation I've heard in recent times is the life of Ted Olbrich. Ted went to Cambodia in 1998 to serve as a missionary. At the time, Cambodia was a devastated nation. In his own words, He describes what he faced when he arrived:

When I came to Cambodia in 1998, the country was

the poorest nation on Earth. The people were lifeless shells, their country devastated after losing one-third of their population to the Pol Pot genocide and disease. I did not know where to start.

The Cambodian people responded to anything material, but not the gospel. I went away to fast and seek the Lord. He gave me a plan that we still use to this day from James 2:18: "But someone will say, 'You have faith, and I have works.' Show me your faith without your works, and I will show you my faith by my works" (NKJV).

Since then, our motto has been: "We will show you our faith by what we do." God always began with a miraculous sign or healing. When the Cambodian people saw us do those works (Isa. 58:6-8), they knew we had more than just "stuff," and they listened. They actually believe they can do what Jesus did.[14]

Today, Ted's ministry, FCOP International is "dedicated to building the kingdom of God through meeting urgent needs and doing good deeds to bring holistic health to a hurting and oppressed people. *We will show you our faith by what we do* (James 2:18b).

From a man who did not know where to begin, there emerged a mission that is literally changing the emotional and spiritual landscape of a nation. The Lord has used one man's willingness to serve a nation to:

+ Plant 6,000 churches
+ Operate 106 church/orphan homes caring for

---

[14] Ted Olbrich. "21 Days of Prayer 2020, Day 11: Faith by Works." The Foursquare Church. https://resources.foursquare.org/day-11-faith-by-works/. Web. 11 January 2020.

3,000 orphans

- ♦ Staff 600 widows to serve the ministry
- ♦ Produce enough rice through farming to feed the children
- ♦ Rescue, train, and equip sexually trafficked young women
- ♦ Provide advanced educational training for qualified orphans
- ♦ Continue to provide family connections and relationships with 18,000 orphans who have been raised in their homes
- ♦ Offer medical and dental teams to remote regions of the nation
- ♦ Provide vocational training and assistance for micro-enterprises

Ted did not know where to start in 1998 when facing such overwhelming need. But God knew; He found a man willing to take the next step and met his obedience in a dramatic and culture-changing fashion.

PRIVATE TO PUBLIC

Recently, I had the opportunity to speak with the leadership team of a church and a group of local entrepreneurs from the business community. I was talking to them about the spiritual environment we create by the quality of life we choose to live. Our private life will eventually have a public influence on the group we serve or the product we create.

I shared the following four points with the group:

1. God prunes us to give definition to our vision and mission. He also redefines us in the pruning. Pruning is never a joyful experience, but it is a critical step in our development. Pruning creates clarity and the potential for an increased harvest.

2. Cutting corners in personal purity and obedience will change our spiritual shape in a negative way both individually and corporately. Compromise is an enemy of faith. Treat it like an unwelcome intruder.

3. Every upgrade in our mission, both personally and corporately, will require that something be left behind if we are going to move forward under the power and freedom of the Spirit.

4. Upgrades do not upgrade our calling or our identity. Upgrades reposition us to see what we could not see about our life and calling before the upgrade took place.

GOD IS INCREASING YOUR SPIRITUAL RANGE OF MOTION

Along with a season of pruning, you might feel like you are being stretched to the breaking point. That's not the goal, nor is it the purpose for what you are experiencing. God is not causing your pain. That is your response to the rigidity and inflexibility He wants to remove. He is using everything in your circumstance to loosen you up and prepare you to move in a new direction. This current season of stretching is designed to increase your spiritual range of motion.

This new range of motion will get stretched again and again as you grow. In the future, it will not appear as daunting as it does at this moment. Your fear will give way to expectation. When challenges arrive, you will be able to reach farther and adapt more easily to the twists and turns they present. You won't break and succumb to fear when an initial pressure and resistance is exerted. You will arrive ready to engage the goodness God has prepared. You will be expectant of something new He wants to accomplish through your increased range of emotional and spiritual motion.

TRUSTWORTHY ENCOUNTERS

Each night, I kneel by our bed and pray for my family that we would have dreams in the night birthed by the Spirit.

One night, I was the recipient of that prayer. In the dream, I was sitting across a table from someone known throughout the world, not only as one of the wealthiest people on the planet but also as a social engineer on a global scale.

He kept looking across the table at me and finally asked, "Would you teach me?" I knew he wanted me to teach him the ways of God.

I told him I would take him to a private place in a forest and teach him, away from inquisitive eyes of those who sought time with him, not as a person, but as a social icon. A public place would put him under unwanted and unnecessary scrutiny. As a result, he would not be able to learn.

When the man asked me to teach him, the Spirit informed me through the unspoken language of dreams that he was actually asking me to train this man in the ways of the Kingdom. The man was free to extend the invitation because he trusted me to protect his identity and not expose him to any jeopardy. I knew the dream was a message for the Church.

God is positioning modern-day Daniels and Josephs, Esthers, and Deborahs next to people of power and influence. If you are one of these people, do not be intimidated by the wealth and power you see. You are not being placed in these opportunities because you have their technical skills or specialized training. You are being placed there because of your anointing that carries the personal and corporate breakthrough these individuals seek.

As these influencers invite you into their world, ask yourself a question: can I be trusted? Can I be trusted to care for the vulnerability and privacy of someone with social influence and not treat them as a trophy? This is a selfie-free zone that needs to remain secret and unadvertised. The interactions that take place in these relationships will carry significant cultural implications. Personal agendas, self-advancement, and unhealthy social alignments will violate this sacred trust. Protect these relationships in an atmosphere of trust.

A BARNABAS MOMENT

In the Arts & Entertainment sphere, people are being touched by God. It seems that with increased frequency, more and more celebrities are coming out and publicly confessing Jesus Christ as Lord. This is a Barnabas moment for the Church.

Some people are concerned with the authenticity of these testimonies. But God asks us to embrace any evidence of faith—even when it's young and still-developing.

When Paul had an encounter with Jesus on the road to Damascus, most people in the Church were afraid of him. It was natural to think Paul was still an enemy and had not changed. I am thankful that Barnabas was willing to stand in the gap and open up the way for Paul to enter into fellowship. That introduction made by Barnabas is still having a profound effect on the Church:

> When he came to Jerusalem, he tried to join the disciples, but they were all afraid of him, not believing that he really was a disciple. But Barnabas took him and brought him to the apostles. He told them how Saul on his journey had seen the Lord and

*that the Lord had spoken to him, and how in
Damascus he had preached fearlessly in the name of
Jesus* (Acts 9:26-27 NIV).

Some of us will be called to step over the lines of
division to embrace those who might carry something
that—if received—will be of great benefit to God's
Kingdom. Barnabas was courageous. His courage
allowed him to bring Saul inside the fearful perimeter
of a persecuted Church, introducing to it a man who
would become one of the greatest apostles in Church
history.

THE AWAKENED CHURCH

Jan and I have shared the same bed for 46 years. We
have learned to discern the subtle difference in each
other's breathing when waking from sleep. Early one
morning, I quietly asked Jan, "Are you awake?" She
replied, "Well, it sounds like you are."

In the natural cycles of sleep and becoming
awakened, we all make unique sounds. The same is
true in matters of the Spirit. The sounds we make will
let those around us know our status of "awake-ness."

Currently, people are using the term "woke" to
describe someone who is socially awake to issues of
justice, discrimination, and human need.

Being "woke" is not a bad idea if we are awakened
to issues that are on God's heart. But if being woke
only means that people share a particular worldview,
they gain very little traction.

A spiritual awakening is taking place. This could be
a woke moment for the Church. But if we choose to
continue living in isolation, fearful of a changing
culture, we will retreat into irrelevance and miss a
tremendous opportunity.

Jesus offered us another option. The awakening we
want to be part of looks and sounds a lot like His

ministry. He gathered twelve people who were not filled with the Spirit and not yet believers—in the traditional sense of the word—and called them to be His first disciples.

To be a disciple is to be a learner. Jesus gave His disciples authority to cast out demons, raise the dead, and perform miracles. All of this took place before they would have fit neatly into our twenty-first-century, evangelical definition of what it means to be a believer.

Jesus did the same thing with the 70, and with anyone willing to learn the ways of Heaven. The early disciples belonged before they believed. They belonged because Jesus invited them to follow Him. He sees people from every walk of life as potential learners who just need someone to give them a chance to taste and see the goodness of God—to belong before they believe.

SUPERNATURAL STRATEGIES

God is resetting us to align with Spirit-empowered strategies. This will lead to the discovery of key relationships, abundant resources, and breakthrough moments. Until a reset happens and a God-alignment takes place, what we attempt to accomplish will remain in the shallow waters of human logic, limited funding, and natural empowerment.

When Jesus gave His disciples instructions for carrying out their commission, His comment followed this introductory note: "But the eleven disciples proceeded to Galilee, to the mountain which Jesus had designated" (Matthew 28:16 NASB).

While I realize Jesus instructed the disciples to go to a physical mountain, the use of the word "mountain" caught my attention in another way. Every one of us has an assignment on one or more the Seven Mountains of cultural influence.

When the disciples arrived on the mountain and

saw Jesus, some of them worshipped and some doubted. On every mountain of influence we stand upon, we will face the same choice: to either worship or to doubt.

The difficult challenges Jan and I have faced brought out all our doubts. What opened the door for breakthrough in those fearful times was an intentional focus on Jesus in an act of worship. We continue to face doubts and ask the Holy Spirit to identify them, in order to acknowledge them as barriers to His love. We identify them as barriers so we can work with God to deconstruct their presence in our lives.

We have a great desire to trust God by continuing to say *yes* to Him whenever we can, especially in the middle of the struggle when we want to do otherwise. At times we have no idea what our next step might be, but a way eventually opens when we say *yes*. Our *yes* becomes an act of worship.

Jesus said, "I have been given all authority in Heaven and on Earth." For every unique Kingdom assignment we have been given and for every obstacle we will face, His authority is present. His authority is our confidence and our *yes*.

THE CLEANUP & SETUP

In a dream, I saw a large conference center. It had just been used to host a gathering of hundreds of people. When the event was finally over, and all the attendees had departed, a stillness settled over the facility. Though it was in good shape structurally, it was messy after the event; the trashcans needed to be emptied and the floor cleaned.

Then I saw a lone janitor quietly working through the empty meeting room. He was enjoying the quiet space and the alone time as he picked up trash, straightened chairs, and swept the floor. He was singing a song as he worked, its melody echoing throughout the emptiness. His song was a prayer. He was at peace even in the task of cleaning such a large space. The peace he carried set the tempo of his life and his response to what surrounded him.

I know the dream had to do in part with a busy season Jan and I had recently experienced. It has a broader application that might apply for some of you who have been running hard and have a lot to clean up. Like us, I invite you to not let the busyness you experienced in the past—or the emotional debris that still clutters your thoughts—to get in the way of the new events that are approaching you. God wants to use this time to prepare you to be ready to receive the next gathering He is bringing your way. Your ability to walk in peace while surrounded by so many things to do will be one of your greatest assets.

Maybe the last season of your life was filled with the execution of essential plans and activities that will someday produce significant fruit. This time of quiet work and reflection has equal significance. In this interlude of cleanup and setup, God will whisper to you what He has planned for the next season. He enjoys this alone time with you as much as He enjoys the events themselves.

CHANGING SEASONS, CHANGING STRATEGIES

I have a group of friends who have invested months of detailed planning into a project with immense potential. The scale of this Kingdom enterprise is global. My friends have done everything they can do, and now comes the waiting. A time of waiting is always filled with emotions.

I recently reminded them that God's word is certain; faith is the only substance they can trust in the waiting. They have done everything with excellence throughout the entire process. They have planted all the seeds. They have shown great integrity, honor, and generosity.

Their product launch will come because God is bringing it to them. They are to stand still and rest and wait for Him to perform His word. Resting and waiting is their action of faith.

I also shared that in order to move into the next phase of the project, they will also need to change roles from that of a seed planter to a midwife preparing for the healthy delivery of their project.

In natural births, midwives are present to calm fears in the delivery, give timely encouragement, provide wise counsel, and help deliver the baby. The same is true for anyone involved in the delivery of a Spirit-birthed and Spirit-empowered Kingdom adventure.

DREAM SEASONS

Dreams and visions have seasons. What worked and brought in a harvest in one season might not work in another. We cannot do what we have always done just because it's what we've always done.

We don't plow in the same way in the same field—season after season—if the field is no longer yielding a harvest. Make sure you know the current season and the gift required to navigate the terrain of that season. There is a time to till the soil, a time to plant the seed, and a time to harvest the fruit. Different seasons will call for different roles. Some new seasons will require a new field.

The Scriptures tell of the Sons of Issachar, who had an understanding of the times, to know what Israel ought to do in the right season (I Chronicles 12:32). Ask God for the wisdom to define your current season, your assigned role in that season, and where you will need to stand at the time of harvest. When the time of fulfillment comes, you will be standing in the right place at the right time.

You will have the honor and privilege of seeing the

purposes of God being birthed before your eyes and get to hold a fulfilled dream in your arms. You will be in awe of the One who first commissioned that dream as a small seed of faith that, against all odds, became a reality.

REGARDING OUTCOMES

The challenging situation you are facing is not as bad as it seems or as good as it can get. You are waiting for something to move one way or the other. You have thought you might be confused or indecisive. You are not.

This is just the way some circumstances unfold. A few things still need to fall into place, and certain people will need to make personal choices before you will see any movement.

No matter which way this goes, God is already present in the outcome with new mercies ready to release. Of all the options you have, trust is the only one that will bring you peace, no matter what happens with the outcome.

UNDERSTANDING THE DETOUR

Take a moment to reconsider the detours that have taken place in your life.

The word "detour" comes from the French word *tourner*, which means "to turn." When God detours you, He is turning your life in a new direction. He is re-routing you through regions of your life and faith you had not previously considered.

In the time of detour, focus on the landscape of God's heart, not on what you are leaving behind or what awaits you. Detours are not designed to rob you of your joy or to destroy your dreams. They are used to reveal the heart of God, and that sight will change the way you view your future and interpret your past.

ANOTHER KIND OF DETOUR

There is a difference between a "God detour" and a dangerous detour.

When life comes to a standstill, not all detours will get you safely around the unexpected delay. Some detours will lead you down perilous paths. There are times when seeking constant forward progress is not the best choice. In these instances, wait for the way to open while cultivating contentment in the delay.

One year we experienced a West Coast winter cyclone similar in strength to a Category 2 East Coast hurricane. The storm brought high winds and dumped loads of snow in our region. Interstate 5 was closed from northern California through southern Oregon. Stranded Thanksgiving travelers turned the closed freeway into a parking lot as they waited for snowplows to clear the way.

Some travelers became impatient and decided to use their GPS to find a secondary road to get around the blocked freeway. One group took a gravel road that is not maintained in the winter, and all of their vehicles became stuck. Finally, after the stranded motorists had been in blizzard conditions for hours, Search and Rescue were able to reach them, saving them from what could have been a tragic incident.

This happens each winter when urban dwellers not used to the reality of winter storms blindly trust a technology like GPS. They put themselves in life-threatening situations. GPS is normally safe in the summer when the roads are dry and clear, but it is an invitation for tragedy in the winter.

We can feel like a traveler on a blocked freeway in a blizzard. A storm of life may have brought our plan to a standstill, and we want to get moving again. We have places to go and people to see. In those stalled seasons, we might start looking for a way around a relationship, a mistake, or a commitment that has delayed a promise.

If this is where you find yourself, hang in there. If God spoke and put you on this path, don't seek another route until He speaks again. The delay in your plans will require patience and trust as the Lord clears the road ahead. Wait for Him. Do not trust your emotional GPS that is luring you onto a side road. The decision to respond only to the voice of God will keep you free of regret and will eventually deliver you safely to your destination.

SPIRITUAL BLIND SPOTS

Just a few miles off the California coast near Santa Cruz, geologists recently discovered a cluster of unknown fault lines on the ocean floor. These seams in the tectonic plate of the planet look like wrinkles on the Earth's crust. What makes this discovery unusual is that this area is one of the most seismically studied parts of the planet. These unseen fault lines are causing concern because of the potential they have for earthquakes and resulting tsunamis. In essence, geologists discovered a tectonic blind spot.

We have similar blind spots. We have a tendency to view the cultural landscape through the lens of our assumptions. When we look at life through the narrow lens of our personal history and biased opinion, we begin to believe our current reality is secure, immovable, and complete when it is really vulnerable and susceptible to change at any moment.

We only see this life in part. Outside our narrow field of vision exists a higher reality that remains hidden in our personal blind spots—hidden until God moves and reveals to us what we did not initially see.

Just as a natural disaster catches people off guard, something similar takes place in a positive way when God moves. The revivals of Church history were not predicted events. Yes, some prophets announced certain aspects of what was to come, but the actual spark point of the revival remained hidden behind a single act of faith. That single act sent tremors through a region, creating a spiritual tsunami that swept across the Church in revival, eventually touching all spheres of culture.

LED BY THE IMPULSE OF GOD'S SPIRIT

Romans 8:5 tells us: "But those who live by the impulses of the Holy Spirit are motivated to pursue spiritual realities" (TPT). The word "impulses" jumped out at me and captured in words what I have been experiencing as I learn how God prompts us to live.

Jan and I—and many of our friends—have sensed a shift taking place in the spiritual realm. While we have tried to live by the impulses of God's Spirit all of our lives, it has become even more vital lately. Living only in response to the impulse of the Spirit will position us to walk more closely with Him, experiencing a deeper oneness and greater sensitivity to what is happening in the world around us.

Our world is filled with impulsive reactions and reasoning. To discern the source of an impulse, we have to step into the protective enclosure of emotional and spiritual rest where God's peace can surround us. He becomes a buffer to the constant onslaught of negative impulsive reactions. We don't want to join a slavish response to every impulsive newscast or advertisement.

When I read about the life of Paul and the other early disciples, I do not see a frenetic form of faith running in all directions responding to each impulse offered by a nervous culture or dysfunctional people. The Early Church lived waiting for the impulse of God's Spirit to direct their steps. They refused to live under the influence of their unsettled emotions and the undisciplined responses of other people.

Today, choose to enter a place of restful waiting and only allow the impulse of God's Spirit to draw you out in response to what is taking place around your life and within culture. This will give you the clarity to lead others in times of cultural stress and discontent.

FINDING OUR PLACE OF REST

Today, one of the most critical decisions any of us will make is the choice to rest. Our greatest peace and our most significant accomplishments come from a place of rest. Without being able to rest, we will create gods in our image. They will become taskmasters beating us down and driving us in submission to something far less than God's best.

Psalm 23:2 reads, "He makes me lie down in green pastures; He leads me beside quiet waters" (NASB). "He makes me lie down" is a familiar and traditional translation for this verse. The original Hebrew could also describe an animal resting with all four legs curled up beneath its body like a deer at rest. Or a mother bird brooding over the chicks under her wings. Or a crouching lion waiting to spring upon its prey. It could even describe sin crouching at the door, waiting to pounce. In all of these possibilities, the subject has chosen the posture of rest, waiting, or crouching.

In order to live in the place and posture of rest described in Psalm 23, we must first lay down the burdens we carry, no longer trying to continually live upright in a posture of self-effort. Someone who chooses a position of rest is no longer able to carry anything.

Some have interpreted the word "make" to mean that God forces us to rest. Psalm 23 is not talking about God forcing anyone to rest if they are unwilling. Have you ever tried to rest when you are driven? Have you gone to sleep without changing the worrisome thought pattern that is causing your sleeplessness? It doesn't work. Here are a few other translations of that phrase:

- ♦ "He lets me rest" (NLT)
- ♦ "He offers a resting place for me" (TPT)
- ♦ "You have bedded me down in lush meadows" (MSG)

We must exchange the weight of our burdens to experience the benefit of rest. God is the only One who can carry our burdens. He will ask us to give Him our need to control a particular outcome, or the desire to control the decision-making process of another person. Control seems to be the issue that creates our "rest-less-ness." When we make that exchange, we will receive back from God the ability to lie down in the green pasture of His rest.

THE ANGEL OF NATIONS

Early one morning while in prayer, I heard the words, "Angel of Nations." I looked toward the front door of our living room and sensed a presence. The veil between Heaven and Earth seemed very thin in that moment, and I knew something was taking place. I could sense, but not see, an angel.

The Lord told me that the Angel of Nations is an angel He sent to help the Church fulfill the Great Commission. This single angel is so powerful he has authority over the principalities and powers that currently control the nations of the Earth.

As I waited in the early morning stillness, I sensed in my spirit this angel was sent to gather nations under his wings as a prophetic sign of his mission on Earth. I believe the Lord allowed me to discern the presence of this angel because of God's timing.

The presence of the angel represented a *karios* moment of heavenly intervention where God was asking us to step up and partner with Him. The Angel of Nations was sent to help us carry out God's plan—the acceleration of the reformation of nations.

Instead of an unfruitful and argumentative confrontation with nations, we will experience a transformation of our mission. Our redemptive efforts will look like the unfolded and inviting arms of a loving Father, not an angry and distant deity. We will see nations stepping into the embrace of God's protective and loving presence and begin to flourish. This ingathering of nations will take place because God has offered them a place of safety and security in a world filled with jeopardy and danger.

Jesus spoke over Jerusalem:

"How often I wanted to gather your children together, the way a hen gathers her chicks under her wings, and you were unwilling" (Matthew 23:37 NASB).

God has always extended that invitation to come and find rest under the wings of His love and mercy.

He is unfolding His divine pathway toward a flourishing future; He desires this for the redeemed and unredeemed alike. That is our commission. It is a Great Commission. In the fulfillment of that calling, the scouts, pioneers, and settlers are being deployed into every sphere of culture under the power and leading of God's Spirit. This is a profound time to be alive.

EPILOGUE: THE REVOLVING DOOR

At the start of this book, I mentioned the discovery of my ancestors in Oregon. That moment is something I now call a "revolving door."

Not long ago, the Lord showed me this idea. I saw myself standing in front of a revolving door. Trying to time my entry, I stepped into the revolving chamber. I also saw someone else walking into the other side of the door going in the opposite direction. I realized I was actually seeing a version of myself from the last season of my life walking into an appointed place in history. When I passed through the revolving door, I stepped into a new season in the Spirit.

Get ready for a change.

What you relied on in the past will no longer provide sufficient support or resource for what God has planned for your future. Your past anointing is being realigned toward a new season and a new assignment.

As you prepare for the journey, leave behind assumptions and stationary thinking. Position yourself at the entry of the revolving door. God will then ask you to take the step of faith required to time your entry into what He is developing.

In this shift—as the revolving door begins to spin— you will experience a moment of amazement and wonder when you see the old version of yourself pass by the new you moving forward. What you learned in the past has taught you a great deal. Nothing will be wasted. But what is coming is even better.

MINISTRY CONTACT

Garris Elkins
Prophetic Horizons
PO Box 509
Jacksonville, Oregon 97530
GarrisElkins.com

Other books by Garris Elkins
available on **amazon.com**:

A Good Place
God-Whispers
The Leadership Rock
Prayers from the Throne of God
The Prophetic Voice
Thoughts to Leave Behind
The Sound of Reformation

Made in the USA
San Bernardino, CA
31 March 2020